What people are saying about …

MISSING JEWEL

'Inspiring. Insightful. Encouraging. A producer, mentor, and treasured friend to many, the wake of Les Moir's life is wide. I'm grateful God moved him to pen this compelling chronicle of the Spirit's work through His people to move His church to worship in Spirit and Truth. In a voice coloured by being both an observer and participator in this history, Les will keep you leaning in for more as he chronicles story after story of the "God-incidences" that ignited and built the modern worship movement in the UK, and far beyond. *Missing Jewel* reminds us that God is always at work, behind the scenes, chiseling the facets of the jewel until it shines for all to marvel at the Glory of the Craftsman and His work.'

Louie Giglio, pastor of Passion City Church, founder
of Passion Conferences, author of *The Comeback*

'The first time I visited the UK was in my early twenties, and to be honest, I felt like I was coming home. The church was rich with life-giving theology, and I was amazed at the array of hymn-like contemporary songs that really spoke to my heart and helped develop my understanding of truthful worship. The global church is far richer for the UK worship movement, who have led the way for my generation in every facet of worship ministry, seen and unseen, and I will ever be grateful. Les Moir has played a significant role in this over many decades, and in my opinion, is the right person to tell this story. Receive and enjoy.'

Darlene Zschech, worship leader and songwriter

'I thought reading through this book would just be a nice exercise in *re-visiting* the past, but something else happened to me along the way—I came away *re-envisioned* for the future. Every page tells a story of God's faithfulness—and how He connects our lives together in beautiful and brilliant ways. I loved reading of the cross-pollination that happened between countries such as Australia, the UK and the USA—and the insight that the key to all this blessing was the rich soil of unity. There's no one better positioned than Les Moir to have written such a book, and it's a fascinating read. More than anything *Missing Jewel* helped me remember that we are *better together*—for there's no question that as worshippers travelling side by side we went much further on this adventure than we could have ever gone alone.'

Matt Redman, worship leader and singer-songwriter

'Les Moir has weaved into a unity the many different strands of the Holy Spirit's renewal of the church's worship, in and through the UK, over the last fifty years. His book parallels my adult lifetime, but I have learned things I did not know, and been reminded of others that I had forgotten. The songs we sing today, and those we will sing tomorrow, do not appear out of nowhere, they are part of a living and deepening tradition, whose story is told here. It is not only those who have loved and sung these songs who will benefit from this book, but anyone concerned with the next part of the story.'

Bishop Graham Cray, chairman of Soul Survivor

'Over the past few decades there have been worship movements that began in the UK and have impacted the church around the world. Songs have been birthed in British churches that are being sung on every continent. Redman, Smith, Townend, Hughes and many others are the faces of this movement. However, the man behind the scenes who has been a father figure, mentor, encourager and enabler is the author of this book, my friend Les Moir. In these pages you will live the story and learn the principles and lessons. Enjoy!'

Mike Pilavachi, Soul Survivor

'Les is one of the most remarkable people I know. Kingdom minded, generous, kind and pure. His ultimate passion is to make the praise of God glorious and he delights wherever he sees this take place. His influence on sung worship in the UK and worldwide is more significant than many of us I think will ever realise. He has continually poured fuel on the flames and championed people unbelievably. He has cheered me on and encouraged me in stunning ways. I simply wouldn't be doing much of what I do today were it not for Les's sacrificial love. I'm so glad he has written this book. A wonderful and insightful look into worship in the church. Everyone loves Les and I'm sure people will love this great book!'

Tim Hughes, worship songwriter and leader of
St Luke's Gas Street Church, Birmingham

'Les Moir does a great job of guiding us through the roots of the modern worship movement in the UK. He's a good guide because he was there through most of it, even playing bass on the original live recording of *Come, Now Is the Time to Worship* in 1998. Because of the two years I lived and worked in the UK training songwriters and worship leaders in the late 90s, I have always felt like an honorary Brit, and I still believe this was one of the most important and fruitful seasons of my life. The chapter on John Wimber and Vineyard Music brought a flood of gratefulness and memories having experienced much of this first hand. If you want to know more about why the UK has had such an important role in renewing worship in song throughout the world, this book is a great start.'

Brian Doerksen, writer of 'Come, Now Is the Time to Worship'

'This book is a fascinating and enlightening story, not just for people like myself who like Les Moir were in the "front row", but also I believe for those whose worship journey and practice has been profoundly shaped by it but have not yet heard it told. Through conversations and interviews with many of the "key players", together with his own personal memories and reflections, Les traces how what became known as "praise and worship" moved from the fringes to the mainstream, to a global phenomenon.'

Graham Kendrick, worship leader and songwriter

'For years, Les has talked about writing this book and I am really delighted that at last he has done so. It is a story, capturing the excitement of the early days of the modern worship movement in the UK; but it is more than that. This book contains insights about the role that sung worship plays in all our lives today. It also looks ahead to an exciting future, encouraging this current generation of songwriters to take the message of God's love beyond the walls of the church, to the whole world.'

Noel Richards, worship songwriter

MISSING JEWEL

THE WORSHIP MOVEMENT
THAT IMPACTED THE NATIONS

LES MOIR

David C Cook
transforming lives together

MISSING JEWEL
Published by David C Cook
4050 Lee Vance Drive
Colorado Springs, CO 80918 U.S.A.

David C Cook U.K., Kingsway Communications
Eastbourne, East Sussex BN23 6NT, England

The graphic circle C logo is a registered trademark of David C Cook.

The website addresses recommended throughout this book are offered as a
resource to you. These websites are not intended in any way to be or imply an
endorsement on the part of David C Cook, nor do we vouch for their content.

All Scripture quotations are taken from the Holy Bible, New
International Version® Anglicized, NIV®. Copyright © 1979, 2011 by
Biblica, Inc.® Used by permission. All rights reserved worldwide.

LCCN 2016961913
ISBN 978-1-4347-1139-7
eISBN 978-1-4347-1163-2

The Cook Team: Ian Matthews, Jennie Pollock, Jo Stockdale,
Nick Lee, Helen Macdonald, Susan Murdock

Cover Design: Mark Prentice, beatroot.media
Cover Images: Adobe Stock
Printed in the United Kingdom by CPI Group (UK) Ltd, Croydon CR0 4YY
First Edition 2017

1 2 3 4 5 6 7 8 9 10

012717

CONTENTS

FOREWORD

Simply, there is no-one like Les.

If Les Moir was a famous footballer, he would have a bronze statue made in his image and it would be placed on Eastbourne seafront for all to see.

But Les is not a footballer; he is the music man.

Simply, he is a man of the music. A man of God.

I was seventeen years old when we first met. I was the new boy at ICC recording studios in the same town, completely green to the culture of a studio but keen to impress and work my way up to one day becoming a sound engineer. Les regularly booked the studio as he was the main record producer of the time, working with Christian artists such as Graham Kendrick, Noel Richards, Phil & John, Chris Bowater and Kensington Temple just to name a few.

I was immediately struck by his sense of focus. He was determined to make the best record he could with often very low budgets. He was absolutely dedicated to his craft and that inspired me. He would not give up; he would work through the night. He would not sleep. He would forget to go home.

One infamous story involved a pint of milk. On a rare day off with his wife, Judith, they had nothing in their fridge. Les was quickly dispatched to go to the corner shop and find some. Many hours later Les returned with the milk but had passed by the studio en route to check two mixes. Why waste a trip to the shop when you can check a mix?

This sense of focus encapsulated everything he did and was the standard for everyone who worked with him. I remember my first project engineering for Les and being shocked at how hard he worked and the sacrifices he made for each artist. Often the space between night and day would be a short nap and it was easier to sleep in my car than travel back to my bedsit.

But Les would always be up early, taking his kids to school and making sure he was being dad to James and Isabel as well as fathering a new movement of worship across the UK. It was chaos amongst the calling.

He was, and is, a kind man and those sessions were full of learning and adventure as we felt we were a part of changing the landscape of Christian music. Each record that was made was a challenge to improve, innovate and explore the sonic boundaries of each new song.

I remember us once listening to a Phil Keaggy record from across the pond and both wondering why it sounded so superior. The drum sound, the guitar tones, the mix through a Neve console. It drove us on to dig deeper and not settle for second best.

Soon Les moved into a different season when he was employed by Kingsway Music to head up their A&R department. Because he was so relational it soon developed into the main European music label that was pioneering the modern move of worship. Matt Redman, Tim Hughes, Soul Survivor, etc. Les was always in the middle of it and still to this day if there is something 'going down' then Les will be there. He has a prophetic nature to him that gave him a keen sense of 'smell' in discovering great new talent but he also had the studio experience to develop artists over a period of time.

I will always be personally grateful to Les for encouraging me endlessly over many years. From listening to my first ever worship song 'Lord You Have My Heart', to giving me my first production job with a young songwriter called Matt Redman-Jones, I think Matt was seventeen and I was twenty … ha!

Even through the Delirious? years when we formed our own record label, Les was always there, cheering from the sidelines, sending messages to keep going or a word of advice about changing the microphone I was using. When we had the dream for CompassionArt he was there, when I need help checking mixes for the Army of Bones, he'll be there.

Prophetic people don't see the boundaries that others see, and Les felt like he was working and supporting every Christian artist even if they weren't on his label! He is a 'Kingdom' person foremost and will always shy away from building his own personal empire.

It's with this experience and unique insight that this book makes such good reading. It's not written by a historian but by someone who was living life amongst the stories in these pages. Reading it made me incredibly grateful for the heroes of the faith who have gone before and pioneered so tenaciously. It's their sacrifice that paved the way for my generation to do what we did, creating new business models like CCLI that helped songwriters earn a living, having a dream for Christian music to be a force in culture not just background music.

People like Les are true heroes.

I think we should build that bronze statue soon.

Martin Smith
January 2017

ACKNOWLEDGEMENTS

Thanks to the late Peter Fenwick and John Pac for the commissioning and opportunity to tell the story.

To Richard Herkes and Clive Price for helping me get started. Craig Borlase—The Storyteller. Sharon Roberts and Steph Bennett for transcribing the many interviews. Sally Johnson for your diligence and eye for detail. Jennie Pollock for making the book better.

JB and Ian for your commitment to Word and Worship. Cross Rhythms for your faithfulness and willingness to share your interviews. Majors Jim and Betty Moir: Legends! My family—Jane, Margaret, Stephen and Heather.

Brother and best man Neil Costello and Julie Costello. Dave Roberts—a friend indeed. Helmut and Elisabeth, Geoff and Jean. Graham and Jill, Juliet and Andy, Dave and Rosie, Dave and Pat. Bryn and Sally—true inspirations and intercessors. Wayne and June Drain for your constant encouragement.

Noel and Tricia Richards for your lion hearts. Tom and Suzie Brock—models of marriage in ministry. Bob and Yvonne Grace for

wise words. Mike Pilavachi my senior consultant. Ben Callander
for teaching me to be a worshipper.

To the Levites of this land—the lineage carries on. Martin and
Anna, Matt and Beth, Tim and Rach, Brenton and Jude, Jorge and
Lucy, Sue Strydom, Adrian and Karen, Doug Williams, Mal Pope,
Rob and Marion Andrews, Marilyn Baker, Noel and Tanya, Bill
and Linda Owen, Lawrence, Faye, Steve and Vel, Bazil Meade and
Mark Beswick. To all those who gave their time to pass on their
part of the story.

The Survivor Stable, Kingsway Crew and the Integrity Team
of Nashbourne and the Abbey Road family.

James and Isabel, I am so proud of you.

Judith, we lived this story and sang 'We are going to fill, fill,
fill the world with music.'

God … you have indeed done great things!

For many of the songs that Les Moir has been involved with
over the years, visit WeAreWorship.com for chord charts, sheet
music and song stories.

Listen to significant songs from the UK worship movement.
Go to www.bit.ly/MissingJewel for a Spotify playlist.

INTRODUCTION

This is not my story but our story. Over the past fifty years God has done an amazing thing in the UK in His church and with worship. As the Holy Spirit was poured out, the British church moved from formality into freedom.

Worship became restored and creativity released. God put a new song in the voice and heart of the church. The teachings, themes and prophetic words were carried into songs and helped shape and build the church.

Near the end of the 1995 Gospel Music Association conference held in Nashville, I was overwhelmed by the high quality of recordings, marketing and performance and was asking myself 'What does the UK have to bring to global Christian music?' On the Sunday morning, before flying home, I was invited to New Song Christian Fellowship, who were then meeting in a school hall.

Michael and Stormie Omartian were ushers that day and greeted me, and I sat in front of Genesis drummer Chester Thompson.

The worship started, and to my surprise three of the four songs were from the UK. I began to realise that God was going to take worship songs from the UK and bless the nations of the world.

As a young recording engineer, I moved to Eastbourne in 1978 to become part of the staff of ICC Studios. My first major project was Graham Kendrick's initial worship album *Jesus Stand Among Us*. I had no way of knowing then what a significant recording this was, in terms of the development and direction of worship music in the UK. During my time at ICC, I was also privileged to record two of the first British gospel albums, *Free at Last* by Maxine and the Majestics and *Changing* by Kainos. I was again honoured to be part of the birth of something new. Under the parental care of Helmut and Elisabeth Kaufmann, ICC became the recording home of Christian/Gospel music in the UK.

I was soon commissioned by Kingsway chief Geoff Shearn to develop the recording of worship albums in the UK. This led me to have the privilege of working with many worship and movement leaders and close to forty years of producing and recording God's music.

In 1992 John Paculabo was appointed as Managing Director for Kingsway Music. He had a dream that the worship songs of the UK would leave the island. Over the twenty years before his death in 2013, he began to see that dream come true; helped by Kingsway's partnership with EMI Christian Music Group (EMICMG) and later Integrity Music, he would see these songs propelled around the world.

Despite the international influence and recognition, the UK worship community continued to be close and would meet together often. The next generation were drawn into the gatherings and the fathers, sons and daughters learned from each other. Pete Greig, founder of 24-7 Prayer, observed that while senior

church leaders have struggled to hand on the baton to the next
generation, the transition between the generations in the UK
worship community has been seamless.

A tapestry of relationships was being woven across the
denominations, streams and movements and God blessed the
unity. David Ruis observes 'I think in the UK there is a deep
passion to find community and that is touching the blessing on
the worship. The pursuit of community and relationship, and
finding ways to cooperate together. I think this is a significant
factor.'

The modern-day Levites of this land care deeply about the
praise of God and have taken seriously their responsibility of
this role.

The UK has such a heritage of hymns. Martin Smith would
say it's 'in the soil'. But the bringing together of majesty and
intimacy and new sounds has seen the combination of content
and creativity leading to encounters with God.

In the writing of this book I have interviewed over fifty key
people who have been involved in, and observers of, this movement, and I have stepped into the role of scribe; a commentator
as well as a collector of quotes. Unless otherwise stated, all quotations are taken from these interviews. This is the story, from
my perspective, of how the jewel of worship was restored to the
British church and went on to become a light to the nations.

> Since my youth, God, you have taught me,
>   and to this day I declare your marvellous
>   deeds.

Even when I am old and grey,
do not forsake me, my God,
till I declare your power to the next
generation,
your mighty acts to all who are to come.
(Ps. 71:17–18)

Chapter 1

THE 1960S—THE EXPLOSION

And then came the 60s.

For the paperback writers and dedicated followers of fashion, the 60s were definitely swinging. But not for the majority of the church. Many were anxious about the nation's downward trend towards permissive values and believed that contemporary culture was best left alone.

So when it came to worship, it was more or less business as usual. Even the seating pattern stayed the same.

Yet the church did experience an explosion of its own. Evangelical Christians were encouraged by stories of thousands who 'went forward' at preaching crusades led by American evangelist Billy Graham. The trouble was, once they left the crusade tent and stepped over the threshold of their local church, all those fresh converts found themselves in an environment that hadn't changed for generations. They shifted from Billy Graham's polished programme, with contemporary sermons and celebrity guests that included a young Cliff Richard, to a foreign evangelical culture lovingly frozen in a formal environment, where hymns like 'And Can It Be?' and 'O for a Thousand Tongues' were the staple diet.

Many loved those old songs. Sung with dedication, they could still move the hardest of hearts. And they had endured too, many of them having travelled beyond church walls and into football grounds ('Abide with Me', 'Guide Me, O Thou Great Jehovah') and school assembly halls ('He Who Would Valiant Be', 'Morning has Broken').

But despite this unique feature of British hymns, the culture gap between church and world was widening. While Wesley and Watts were still gracing the hymn board, Lennon and McCartney were changing the face of popular music. According to worship leader and modern hymn-writer Graham Kendrick, both had their influence: 'Every Sunday I would be in church singing the traditional hymns, then listening to the Beatles when we got home. When people ask me who my inspirations are, I typically say, the Beatles and the Baptist Hymnbook!'

Even though hymns were often sung with great gusto at the livelier end of the evangelical spectrum, worship was generally regarded as songs sung to warm up the congregation for the sermon. It was a preliminary to the preaching.

American preacher A.W. Tozer was among those troubled by an apparent imbalance in the church's spiritual diet. Tozer's ministry flourished in the fifties in the Chicago area, from where he edited the *Alliance Weekly* magazine. His articles were compiled into booklet form, one of them called *Worship: The Missing Jewel in the Evangelical Church*. Published in 1961, it made the claim that modern evangelical praise didn't come anywhere near the standards set by the Old Testament worshippers, with their choirs, drums, flutes, and general burst of creativity. His observation was spot on: 'It is certainly true that hardly anything is missing from our churches these days—except the most important thing. We are missing the genuine and sacred offering of ourselves and our worship to the God and Father of our Lord Jesus Christ.'[1]

Tozer's challenge was a serious wake up call to the church. It was time to return to its primary calling; love the Lord your God with all your heart.

God was about to do something extraordinary, something that would see this precious jewel of worship being rediscovered and restored to its rightful place. From the early 1960s a number of men and women, in both independent churches and established ones, became involved in what turned out to be one of the biggest renewal movements in history.

It all began with thousands being filled with the Holy Spirit. Such powerful spiritual encounters radically transformed their view of worship. They split churches and sparked off many a heated debate in the wider church. But they also rejuvenated many people's relationship with God and understanding of Him.

Michael and Jeanne Harper were among them. Michael was a curate with world-renowned Anglican Bible teacher John Stott, based at one of the 'capitals' of evangelicalism, All Souls, Langham Place in central London. While preparing to teach on the book of Ephesians, Michael experienced the reality behind the apostle Paul's prayer that the saints in Ephesus would be strengthened by the Holy Spirit.[2] Michael received so much of the fullness of God that he had to ask God to stop giving him more. He returned home full of joy—leaving his wife wondering how to cope with a transformed husband.

At that time Michael was also chaplain to some of the shops on London's busy Oxford Street. A young backslidden Christian named John Noble was working at a department store there and ended up attending a lunchtime service led by Michael. The Harpers reached out to John and his wife Christine, and eventually the couple committed their lives to God afresh. John also had an experience of the Holy Spirit: 'I was so touched by the Spirit that I was crying and weeping and walking around praying for my friends without any inhibition.'

This outpouring of the Holy Spirit was also affecting the worship at churches on Sundays. Terry Virgo, a young pastor at Vale Road Evangelical Church in Seaford, who eventually became a leading figure in the charismatic movement, recognised something had changed, even though the songs remained the same: 'While singing old hymns at church, people would start putting their hymnbooks down halfway through the last verse. It had become so formal, but this was different—people wanted to tell God how much they loved him. I'd never known anything like it before. You felt a motivation to worship, a fresh love and intimacy—and a sense of the immediacy of God's presence—which drew out worship from your heart in an unprecedented way.'

Driven by fresh encounters, they believed they were enjoying an increased intensity of the Holy Spirit—just as the early church had done in the book of Acts, which they were now reading with fresh urgency.

Many people were beginning to find it virtually impossible to be formal in their worship. Rather than proclaim grand doctrinal statements via faithful and familiar hymns, they now wanted to direct new expressions of love towards heaven.

Terry Virgo saw the impact: 'Worship began to be restored, simply because we were enthused with Jesus and thrilled with the Holy Spirit. I don't think we were consciously thinking that we needed to restore worship. I just think we started worshipping.'

Jeanne Harper eventually shared in her husband's experience, and in 1971 the couple went on to form the Fountain Trust. As an interdenominational attempt to encourage 'local churches to experience renewal in the Holy Spirit', the Fountain Trust helped to spearhead charismatic renewal within the Anglican church. Michael started to hold meetings, with Jeanne leading worship on piano:

> When I was baptised in the Spirit I had Charles Wesley hymns beside my bed and Michael had John Wesley's journals. We tried to get the unedited versions of Charles Wesley's hymns, because any allusions to the Holy Spirit or to feelings had been taken out. We did find that the worship grew, and the songs would express what the Holy Spirit was doing in people's hearts.
>
> I suppose we were very Anglican. Michael would be the priest and we would have a lot of silences during our worship. I would be at the piano and start to play something quietly, and he would sense it was right and off we'd go. The

worship times became quite extensive. We were
absolutely over the moon with God.

John Wimber, who was a major influence in the UK church,
said in an interview with *Worship Together* magazine that histori-
cally every move of God has produced new music.[3] Sometimes the
music actually precipitated revival, sometimes it occurred during
revival, but music was always present in the aftermath. The new
songs of the renewal were soon to be heard.

Interestingly, just as the charismatic movement began to find a
foothold in Britain, a new wave of creativity was hitting the island's
shores, impacting the nation's youth as it did. It came via a young
Glaswegian called Lonnie Donnegan.

Lonnie was the unsung hero of the 60s' explosion of pop
music. He inspired hundreds of teenagers to start playing the guitar, and thousands of musicians all over Britain got their first taste
of music through him and the skiffle music he played. It gave them
hope. Years later, band leader Chris Barber claimed that Lonnie
Donnegan had had a far greater influence on the development of
rock music in Britain than the Beatles had ever had.[4] It was Lonnie
who inspired Paul McCartney to become a musician and songwriter and John Lennon formed his first group, The Quarrymen,
after listening to Lonnie's records.

Joy Webb, founder of the Salvation Army group The Joystrings
was caught up in it: 'It was one of the summers of skiffle … an
upsurge of pure home made music making. It seemed anyone
could do it—and did! Every available tea chest in the country
was commandeered as a substitute for a double bass. I plunged

headlong into the new music with a beat. The Salvation Army had a veritable treasure chest of singable songs and choruses which adapted well into skiffle.'[5]

After Salvation Army General Frederick Coutts told the press about the new music coming out of his organisation, Joy was commissioned to pull together a group of girl singers who played a little guitar to appear at short notice on the *Tonight* programme for the BBC in December 1963. They went down well and were invited back by popular demand, this time complete with two male cadets, Bill Davidson and Peter Dalziel.

It was this appearance that was caught by a top executive of the giant EMI company, and before long they recorded the song 'It's an Open Secret'. It became an instant success. Reaching number thirty-two in the pop charts, it stayed there for seven weeks.

The success of The Joystrings was an inspiration to the many Christian groups that had been formed. But it was about more than fame and recognition; there was now an underground circuit of coffee bars being used for evangelism. There was a new tribe of musicians and artists diving into this culture and embracing the creativity that emerged within it, at the same time that they were experiencing a fresh outpouring of the Holy Spirit on His church. Something new was about to be birthed.

A group of young men in their twenties, who would go on to play a very significant role in the Christian youth revolution in the 60s and 70s, was about to emerge. Pete Meadows, Geoff Shearn, Dave Payne and John Webb were united in their quest for something fresh and vibrant. In time, they would inspire an entire movement of young Christians.

Pete and Dave were in a band called The Unfettered while Geoff was part of a band called The Envoys. In a remarkable God-incidence, Pete and Geoff were travelling in the same lift when Pete noticed that Geoff was wearing a Scripture Union badge. They started talking and Pete invited Geoff to a lunchtime fellowship that he and Dave had set up. The group was inspired by the work of an American evangelist, Bill Bartham, who started an organisation called Network which organised youth events in coffee bars.

Pete and Dave would travel to a town, decorate the church hall to look like a coffee bar, and advertise around the streets. They'd sing the gospel to people, but using rock music. They called it coffee evangelism and it created a circuit where many of the bands would play, allowing musicians to bump into each other. Pete started to organise day events which built into a significant conference in Swanwick where 2–300 musicians, artists and poets turned up. He also organised retreats for bands.

Dave was the deal maker and management type while Pete, and now Geoff, were creative and came up with new ideas and concepts. Pete had a flair for marketing while Geoff gravitated towards musical creativity and was better with money than anyone else. John Webb had a vision to hear a Christian voice expressed on radio and looked after the admin side of things. Together they formed Musical Gospel Outreach (MGO), to help bridge the gap between evangelism and contemporary culture.

John Paculabo, known to everyone as 'John Pac', was a young musician from Liverpool with an Anglican church background, who experienced MGO at first hand.

For me the inspirational times were between '67 and '69 when MGO called all Christian musicians to Swanwick in Derbyshire. We didn't know anything about the people; all we knew was that there was going to be a Christian concert and some friends and I decided that we wanted to be there because we didn't have any peers, apart from a few groups in our locality. In those days many of the ministers were really against youth starting bands because they saw it as part of the pop culture and the dangers that went with that.

We went along and it was jam-packed. I remember seeing a couple of funny guys called Ishmael and Andy. The most amazing UK talent in those days was Judy McKenzie who herself was very inspirational and wrote what I thought were incredible songs for that period of time. She was the first Christian artist who I thought had the ability to go and stand on the stage and hold an audience on her own with just a guitar. Graham Kendrick was also around at that time, with a band called Whispers of Truth. They performed at Swanwick and I could see he had a talent for writing.

It was a fun time. Here we were, just a bunch of try-hards from all over—Scotland, the south coast, east and west—encouraging each other and learning from each other.

At one point Pete Meadows held up a sheet
of A4 and said that it was going to be the news-
letter and that they were going to call it Buzz.
It went on to become an exhaustive, informative
magazine for anyone involved in Christian music
or even anyone wanting to book a band for a
coffee bar event.

Graham Kendrick recalls: 'I feel in the MGO times there was
a release of creativity right across the church, suddenly it was ok to
play an acoustic guitar and to be more casual. It seemed like a new
day from before as we transitioned from church organ to acoustic
guitar.'

As MGO was growing in confidence, so were Christian musicians—even Christendom itself. When Billy Graham announced
that Cliff Richard was to join him on stage at a crusade in Earls
Court, the crowds flocked. The venue filled and 5,000 people
were turned away as Cliff, who was at his prime as a rock 'n' roll
artist, announced his conversion to Christianity. He sang 'It Is No
Secret', a gospel song which Elvis Presley had recorded, and when
the meeting ended Cliff went outside to address the thousands
who hadn't been able to get in. Cliff had become the most famous
British Christian who was also a rock 'n' roll singer; this helped
dispel any issues in terms of the compatibility of singing rock 'n'
roll and being a Christian.

Beyond the walls of the church, these were the days of drugs
and mysticism, and Christianity was not a cool religion for a pop
star to embrace. For Christian musicians the sight of Cliff on stage

with Billy Graham shattered the illusion that contemporary music could not be used in church. After all, as Cliff went on to sing when he covered the Larry Norman song, 'Why Should the Devil Have All the Good Music?'

Meanwhile, in youth group meetings up and down the country new songs were being sung. Many were found in *Youth Praise*, a 150-strong songbook that had become a highly successful and significant series, especially in the more orthodox denominational churches. Compiled by Michael Baughen (who served as rector at All Souls, Langham Place) and assisted by Richard Bewes, *Youth Praise* existed 'for the provision of words and tunes in adequate number and variety to allow contemporary expression of youth praise and worship'. It allowed a whole generation of musicians to hone their skills accompanying these songs, among which were 'Can It Be True?', 'Jesus Is the Saviour' and 'Walking in the King's Highway'.

Michael remembers:

> It was 5 March 1966, the atmosphere was electric; there was a sense of excitement in the packed Westminster Central Hall. A Christian songbook for young people called *Youth Praise* was being launched. No longer confined to hymns and children's choruses; no longer accompanied just by organ or piano. The instrumentation for the evening was two guitars, a banjo, a set of drums and an enthusiastic youth choir. Cliff Richard was interviewed by David Winter.

CSSM (Children's Special Service Mission, which was later to become Scripture Union), had successfully brought out a chorus book for children but not for youth. After compiling a potential collection of songs, I trekked round the main evangelical publishers. They all told me it would be a failure, that there was no demand for such a book. But then Timothy Dudley Smith, who was Assistant Secretary for CPAS (Church Pastoral Aid Society), agreed to publish it. The book swept around the country and overseas. Modern hymn writer Keith Getty says *Youth Praise* was a huge influence on him.

In the months that followed the launch we began to be inundated with new songs from around the country and we realised we would need to have a *Youth Praise 2*. We also got into writing and composing with vigour. The enthusiasm for *Youth Praise* meant that we were able to take the Royal Albert Hall for the launch of *Youth Praise 2* in November 1969, and had to take it for the afternoon as well because of the overwhelming demand. Richard Bewes led 100 guitars and it was amazing to be there and to think back to our early thoughts of a Christian youth songbook.

A new ministry called Scripture in Song also emerged. Led by David and Dale Garratt from New Zealand, it started to impact the UK church, especially those entering Renewal. By looking to the Bible for lyrics, Scripture in Song offered these churches an effective solution to the problem of introducing new songs to well established church services. After all, it was extremely difficult for anyone to take a negative position against the singing of Scripture.

Barney Coombs, leader of the Basingstoke Community Church (formerly Basingstoke Baptist Church), was very connected in terms of the international church, and would bring people in, as well as songs, that he felt would bless the British church. Barney heard David and Dale's songs in New Zealand and brought them back to the UK.

Terry Virgo remembers, 'For me, the first move on from the hymns and the Redemption songbook was probably beginning to hear the Scripture in Song choruses, which I thought were just beautiful. That was new music altogether. Just scripture set to music. I would say they were probably the first new songs I heard. The choruses we were singing were old Elim choruses, these new songs of Scripture began to affect our worship quite a bit.'

Scripture in Song recordings came into the UK through Anchor Recordings, run by Peter Wallis, who was closely connected to Youth With A Mission (YWAM). This was distributed by mail order service and was independent, but it became quite significant. Peter Fenwick, then Chairman of Kingsway, would call Scripture in Song 'The YWAM music'.

When the Garratts had recorded their first home-spun extended play record twenty-five years earlier they had had no idea that it would take off around the world and set the pace for a

whole new wave of songwriters and worship leaders influencing
the shape of church worship everywhere. David Garratt said that
he thought this record would be particularly helpful to people
living in rural parts of New Zealand unable to enjoy worship in
larger city churches. The international response to his music was a
complete surprise to him.

Nigel Coltman was the manager of the Christian bookshop
in Bromley at the time. He remembers: 'Almost out of nowhere
Scripture in Song happened. The house church movement loved it.
It was their kind of music. We were just selling dozens and dozens
a week of "Prepare Ye the Way" and "Thou art Worthy"—the first
two tapes that came out. I couldn't believe it but more and more
people started to use those in house churches and prayer groups.'

Graham Perrins, editor of the most influential charismatic
magazine of the time, *Fullness*, and a gifted Bible teacher on worship and the prophetic, introduced worship leader Wayne Drain to
New Zealand, where he met David and Dale. Wayne observed that
David and Dale were like father and mother to the worship community there. They were very pastoral to the musicians alongside
mentoring them in worship.

When Brian Houston, founding pastor of Hillsong in
Australia, was asked by *Worship Leader* magazine which leaders had
inspired him the most, he cited David and Dale:

> My wife and co-pastor, Bobbie, was born again in
> a thriving church on the main street in Auckland,
> New Zealand, in the 1970s. The church had huge
> momentum as a result of the Jesus Revolution,

and they had a strong emphasis on worship. David and Dale led the Scripture in Song, which at the time was a real pioneering way of doing church music. The way they brought spirit and life and passion to what was traditionally just choruses and hymns, inspired me. I always believed in the potential of the local church and encountering that kind of worship stirred in me a dream to inspire others and change the way people sang in church.[6]

Scripture in Song also served to ignite worship music in Calvary Chapel churches in California, which birthed Maranatha Music. Maranatha was one of the main purveyors of the 'praise music' label and carries that banner even today. Songs such as the classic 'Seek Ye First' and 'I Love You, Lord' became the anthems of an entire generation of believers who came to Christ during this time.

But perhaps the most significant change in 1968 was prompted by the meeting of John Noble and Maurice Smith. John—who had been brought up in the Salvation Army—was now a house church leader in Essex. Growing up, John had heard revival stories from grandparents on both sides of his family. 'As a child, my favourite meeting of the week was what they called the Wind Up, which was after the Sunday evening service. We all stayed behind and really got going with songs and spontaneity with testimonies. So when I came to lead a church I was very happy with spontaneous worship and encouraging people to sing. This played a strong part right from the start.'

Maurice, meanwhile, had started a splinter group from the Baptist Church and was now based in Canterbury. He had a reputation for always being somewhat ahead of his time, and had spent time with a group in Chard, Somerset, where a joy-filled charismatic meeting was taking place:

> I shall never forget my first visit to Chard. The morning was in full swing when we walked in, and I had never heard anything like it in my life. I was running a sort of fellowship in Canterbury, which we thought was a pioneering situation with some elders. Our thing was dead compared with Chard. It was the noisiest thing I've ever heard.
>
> It was run by Sid Purse and his wife, [known to all as] Aunt Mill. All this leaping and danc-ing and shouting was going on, then someone would prophesy. The incredible worship was out of this world.

Driving back to Canterbury, Maurice called in on John Noble, telling him all about what he had seen. Inspired, John and Maurice, along with good friends Graham Perrins, Gerald Coates and George Tarleton, decided to do something similar. They started to hold meetings in the Leprosy Mission Hall in north London. These gatherings were all male and they became affectionately known as the London Brothers, which included notable songwriters such as Dave Bilbrough and Ian Traynar.

According to Gerald Coates, the meetings were unique. 'Maurice, John Noble, myself and others began to gather leaders. They were remarkable times of loud praise, passionate prayers and prophetic ministry, even though they were by invitation only. We had to keep moving venues as our numbers kept growing.'

Terry Virgo was among those attending. 'The first thing I noticed was the exuberance of the worship. I hadn't seen such enthusiasm in worship since Buckingham Street, where the leaders of the emerging house church movement gathered. They were exciting people to be around.'[7]

In *Restoring the Kingdom*, Andrew Walker says: 'The house church movement began to accelerate throughout the UK. The house church movement is the largest and most significant Christian formation to emerge in Great Britain for over half a century. Not since the Pentecostal movements of Elim and the Assemblies of God were established in the late 1920s had such a distinctive and indigenous Christian grouping arrived on the religious scene.'[8]

Interestingly, up to this point the worship at events was generally led by the person fronting the meeting, not necessarily a musician, so at many of these gatherings Maurice would adopt an approach similar to the one he had seen in Chard. He had a special *Redemption Hymnal*, with a list in the back of choruses and other worship songs that he could lead the congregation in. Maurice's main emphasis was on being in the flow of the Holy Spirit, which suited his intuitive nature, and he would pick songs spontaneously.

A new style of beautiful worship was emerging in the body of Christ—genuinely expressing the breath of fresh air that was coming from the house church movement. Scripture in Song had been the pace setter, but now the British were beginning to make a contribution. Soon the groundbreaking worship album *A Door of Hope* (1975) came along from Mavis and Loxley Ford and Chris Head, from the North London Community Church. The album included the song 'Jesus, How Lovely You Are' written by Dave Bolton. Recording engineer Helmut Kaufmann says that this group, calling themselves The Valley of Achor, 'were the first British group that moved away from performance, to worship and praise to God.'

They had sent Kingsway a cassette of twenty of their songs, of which twelve were chosen to be recorded. Chris Head says, 'It was home grown innocence'. Recorded over a weekend at ICC Studios, it was produced by John Pantry, and Chris played bass and guitar. Dave Bolton was invited to lead 'Jesus, How Lovely You Are' at a Westminster Central Hall event, propelling the song into the wider church. The album's artwork helped set it apart and it looked beautiful on vinyl.

Other significant songs (including 'We'll Sing a New Song of Glorious Triumph' by Diane Fung), began to come from Cornerstone, a vibrant, fast-growing church in Southampton led by Tony Morton. David Mansell wrote a majestic song, 'Jesus Is Lord (Creation's Voice Proclaims It)', which rapidly became almost the anthem of the charismatic movement. It was being sung everywhere and was the first classic hymn to come out of the recent move of the Holy Spirit.

These were the exciting 60s, but not for the reasons making the mainstream news. The truth was that the Holy Spirit was being poured out. There was an explosion of creativity. A new generation of leaders was stepping up. And to complete the decade, a praise song made it all the way to the top of the charts.

The Edwin Hawkins Singers went to number one in 1969 with Edwin's arrangement of a centuries-old standard from the Baptist Hymnal, 'Oh Happy Day'. Featuring the lead vocal of Dorothy Coombs Morrison, it went on to sell seven million copies worldwide and become a history-making recording.

It also resonated with the growing Caribbean population that had arrived in the UK over the previous twenty years, beginning with the arrival of West Indians on the SS Empire Windrush which had docked in the UK in June 1948, 'carrying with it the hopes and dreams of hundreds of young men and women. The ship's arrival signalled a moment of historic transformation: the beginning of the mass migration which was to have such far-reaching effects on Britain over the next half-century.'[9]

As a new decade came into view, some wondered whether this was a blueprint for the future of church music; an ever-increasing presence in the mainstream charts. God, however, had other plans.

Chapter 2

THE 1970S—COMING TOGETHER

Another explosion was on its way. This time it was a massive revival which started in California; the Jesus Movement.

It was remarkable, with some estimates suggesting that more than 800,000 young people came to Christ within a year and a half. And it made a massive impact on the sounds coming out of the church. Many of these young, hippy converts were rock musicians, and the Jesus Movement led to the birth of bands like Love Song and The Second Chapter of Acts, as well as the rise of solo artists like Larry Norman. These artists would become major pioneers in contemporary Christian music.

Now baby boomers not only had Jesus, but they also had a church that was indigenous to them, with the music to prove it.

It was not long before the music headed east across the Atlantic. Among the first was Larry Norman, who was accompanied by an evangelist called Arthur Blessitt, who carried an eight-foot cross around the country. Their many trips together helped fan the flame of creativity and evangelism across the UK.

FESTIVAL OF LIGHT

In November 1970 missionary couple Peter and Janet Hill returned to England to live after a four-year stint in India. Peter (who had been a Bishop in India) and Janet were shocked by the growing trends in the mass media for the explicit portrayal of sexual and violent themes. They shared their concern about the state of the country with others, prayed and had a vision of angels over Trafalgar Square with thousands and thousands of people packing onto the streets below.

Peter wanted to set up something called AMP—About Moral Pollution—but Malcolm Muggeridge, a journalist and broadcaster who had found faith in his early sixties, told him that instead of majoring on the negative of moral pollution, what the country really needed was something positive.

The idea took shape, and Peter and Janet's vision became the Festival of Light. The plan was both to petition the government about the terrible things happening in the country and to call the church to stand up together for righteousness.

In the build-up Peter and Janet took to the road, visiting church leaders, members of parliament and trade union leaders. With Malcolm Muggeridge's help, the Festival of Light was launched on Saturday, 25 September 1971. It was less than a year since Peter and Janet had returned from India, but an eclectic group of national leaders stood upon the vacant fourth plinth of Trafalgar Square in front of 30-35,000 people. The entire crowd then marched to Hyde Park for an evangelistic concert where an extra 50,000 people joined in the bold witness to the Lordship of Jesus.

In the months that followed marches were carried out throughout the nation. Never before in the church in the British Isles have so many Christians demonstrated so boldly their faith and concerns. In time, the Festival of Light became CARE, the Christian advocacy group.

Musician John Pac was at the Festival of Light and was moved and inspired by the event:

> Just to see so many people who were interested in goodness and purity had quite an impact on me. I was in a band called Trinity Folk [who later would be called Parchment] and we had no sooner come back from the festival than my fellow band member Sue McClellan began to write the song 'Light Up the Fire'. A few of us shaped it, and when we played it the following spring at Coventry Cathedral, John Webb—who was one of the founding members of Musical Gospel Outreach—came up and said, 'Do you realise what you have done? You've just written this year's festival song!'

Mastering engineer Denis Blackham, who was then working at the established IBC recording studios, became involved in the project.

> MGO executive Geoff Shearn came in and said he had a band called Parchment that he wanted to record a single with and wondered if I knew a record producer who would be interested. The

senior engineer at the time was John Pantry, who
came from a Christian background although he
wasn't a Christian as such, so I recommended
him. The next thing I know John was asking me
if the studio was available to record the single.
It was recorded in one weekend and went on
to become number thirty-one in the national
BBC charts. It wasn't too long after that that
John became a Christian. In time he went on
to produce and develop many Christian artists.

John Pac learned a lot from John Pantry. 'He was a great
producer who turned "Light Up the Fire" into something that
was really memorable. In those days he was the Christian George
Martin, and he taught us so much and he had some great ideas.
This was the first time I'd really stepped into a recording studio.
Even the smell of the place made an impact on me and I knew that
it was what I wanted to do for the rest of my life: to be involved in
recording and music and recording studios.'

John Pac would go on to produce hundreds of albums himself,
but credited John Pantry as 'a great teacher even if he didn't set out
to teach you. You just learned by watching and listening.'

Having recorded 'Light Up the Fire', Parchment got a deal
with Pye Records and the song was given a mainstream release just
before the Festival of Light in 1972, thus lifting the profile of the
song and the festival. Parchment played the song live, and hearing
75,000 people in Hyde Park singing it made a lasting impact on
John Pac and the band.

'Light Up the Fire' remained a popular song, still used in many schools for decades after. In his book *Walk On: The Spiritual Journey of U2*, Steve Stockman describes Bono's time at the Mount Temple school and the barbecues on the beach at which Bono was known to do a campfire version of the song.

MGO soon discovered the importance of music publishing. They had formed a record label called Key Records, to produce recordings for their bands, but had no mechanism for promoting the songs, collecting royalties and managing copyright issues. All that was handled by external publishing companies. Geoff Shearn and the rest were on a steep learning curve. 'Initially we had no real idea about publishing. It just seemed wrong that some third party publisher was collecting revenue where we were committed to actively promoting the artists and their songs.' They started to look into rectifying this.

John Pac was also aware of these discussions, especially when he took part in a Sound Vision concert at Westminster Central Hall.

> It was one of an early series of concerts promoted by Key Records. Making my way backstage, I was met by Pete Meadows who grabbed me by the arm and whispered 'You'll love this—we're going to call the publishing division Thankyou Music'.
>
> His broad, ear-to-ear grin made it impossible for me to not respond enthusiastically (although I did think it was a great name). In years to come Thankyou Music would carry songs around the world, and find translations in many nations.

COME TOGETHER

It all started in 1971 with a simple suggestion over a meal in California. 'Why don't you write a musical about our church?' pastor Jack Hayford had asked his guests. Jimmy and Carol Owens—Christian composers and key figures in the Jesus Movement in America—liked the idea, and within hours had the seeds for Come Together; a production that was to revolutionise worship on both sides of the Atlantic.

The story of how it crossed from America to the UK is worth telling. Enter Jean Darnall, an American speaker and church leader, who had lived in England for twenty-five years and was to play a very prominent role in the next stage of the missing jewel of worship being restored. Before moving to the UK, Jean had been on the leadership team of Jack Hayford's church, The Church on the Way, on the outskirts of Los Angeles. Once Come Together was up and running (and benefitting from the involvement of Christian pop star Pat Boone), Jack contacted Jean, saying that he felt strongly that she ought to meet with Jimmy and Carol.

At a breakfast meeting with Jimmy and Carol, Jean (who was in North America for some speaking engagements) heard all about Come Together, which was being put on by churches across America, with each congregation providing its own worship leader and musicians. And when she saw it she knew that Jack was right. 'It was exactly the message that God was giving us in England. It was a way of ministering to the Lord in worship, ministering to one another in the church and ministering to the world, too, which was the great theme that the Holy Spirit was emphasising in the charismatic movement.'

Back in England she showed the promotional film for Come Together to some friends.

> They said that it was very moving and inspiring but it was too American, with people raising their hands and forming little groups to pray for one another. It was unheard of in England, even with charismatic renewal. They told me that the church wasn't in that place of worship yet. I said that I didn't think it was American; I thought it was the Holy Spirit. I remember coming back home I told my husband Elmer that everyone liked it but no one was motivated to do it. He said, 'Well, I guess you are to do it.' I reminded him that I am not a musician or worship leader but he said if I had the vision for it I should do it.

At a similar time, Barney Coombs was visiting Canada, and reports 'I was preaching at a FourSquare church, and a guy said to me "I want you to listen to this", I listened to the recording of Come Together. I was concerned that we didn't drop the ball in England, here was something that could gather the nation together.' On his return to England, Barney got in contact with Jean Darnall, who he knew from the Festival of Light, and teamed up with her to work on it.

A friend named Terry Sanderson encouraged Jean to pray and ask the Lord where He wanted her to take Come Together. By now it was 1973, and the UK was being rocked by sex scandals involving government ministers. The country was in crisis, and the Lord gave Jean a list of ten cities, starting with Edinburgh. Pat Boone came over and fronted the tour, supported by local church musicians. They started at the Usher Hall, Edinburgh, with Jean knowing that if the musical could break through the reserve of the Scottish church, it would work anywhere. 'You could hear this murmur of prayer going on and the place was packed, with standing room only. It just took off from there.'

As Ralph Turner expands in his biography of Gerald Coates: 'Gerald added his considerable energies to the administration skills of Jean Darnell and Peter Lyne, a facilitator and church leader who was well connected. Along with others, they took it to the nation. David Taylor, Gerald's fellow leader at Cobham Christian Fellowship, also contributed, managing the day-to-day administration of the tour.'[1]

The musical united many diverse churches and gave strength to the nation. Multitudes came together to worship. In Birmingham they turned away as many as were admitted due to lack of space. The same thing happened in Belfast where, for the first time since the start of the troubles, Protestants and Catholics came together with priests and laity pledging themselves to reconciliation.

Crusade magazine, which was the main monthly Christian publication at the time, wrote that Come Together had done more for the spiritual life of the church than any other event in the previous fifty years. It was a breakthrough point and God's hand was on it. Nobody else could take the credit; it was a sovereign love of God to the church.

Gerald Coates was at the performance of Come Together at Westminster Central Hall:

> I was actually running up the stairs when the first few bars opened up and I just burst into tears. I knew intuitively this was going to be a big move of God, and of course the songs went around the nation. It was done by lots of people all over the country after Pat Boone had gone, and became a training ground for young worship leaders.
>
> There was an informality and freedom to Come Together, without it becoming frivolous or sacrilegious, and with a strong emphasis on keeping order. Some people may have clapped hands before, but many had never raised their arms. Come Together changed all that. Many people found a new freedom in their style of worship and promoted the use of contemporary songs as well as older hymns in church services.
>
> Out of that came waves of initiatives and other spin-offs that were happening at a local church level. So much Christian music was released at that time too, not to mention the start of the house church movement and the rise of Holy Trinity Brompton in Knightsbridge.
>
> Come Together was probably one of the key things that followed the Jesus Movement. It brought together people from across the denominations to

worship and to pray. It may have been in a more conservative fashion then, but it was very, very key.

With 30,000 people gathering in Trafalgar Square for the Festival of Light in 1971, and Come Together igniting churches across the country in 1974, the ground was being prepared for a dramatic change.

Like others, Terry Virgo could see the impact of Come Together:

> It was a tremendous vehicle because it didn't just have beautiful music and great songs; it taught that we come to worship and minister to one another. That was the sort of church we were wanting to build in our local congregations, and we were looking for participation, not just going to church to look at the back of someone's head in the pew in front. Come Together reflected the idea that He is here, He is moving among us as we gather in His name. It helped take us forward and gave high visibility to some of the things we were trying to work out locally. Even in a big meeting they'd found a way of praying for one another and ministering to one another. I think it was an excellent contribution.

Graham Kendrick was also impacted. 'Come Together turned out to be a powerful influence on British churches. Despite the sentimental ballads, it's safe to say that it literally changed the way we worshipped and brought Christians together from across the older denominational divides. This was an exciting time when a lot seemed to be happening around the place—lots of tours and events, and people doing new things.

For John Pac the musical 'was really the beginning of the praise and worship movement,' while for Dave Fellingham the whole event was the first time he had seen what we now recognise as contemporary worship: 'It had huge impact. There were great songs like "Freely, Freely; Holy, Holy" that are still in our repertoire now, as well as round singing, antiphonal singing, hand clapping and a congregational dynamic with raising hands and shouting.'

Around the same time that Come Together was touring the country, Spree 73—a large scale youth event—took place at Earls Court. This period was a uniquely exciting time, and many felt inspired to experiment creatively, especially when they saw Musical Gospel Outreach bringing in people like Larry Norman from the States and booking significant venues such as the Albert Hall.

Things had also started to develop in other ways at MGO. The guys had met Bob McKenzie, who worked for an American record label called Benson. Bob always had time to encourage the Brits and came to England regularly to record different sessions. He got involved in the MGO Swanwick conferences and offered to help develop British artists by recording one or two of their tracks at the end of his sessions. MGO were struck by Bob's sheer professionalism and saw an improvement in the quality of their recordings.

Thanks to Bob's help with Graham Kendrick's album *Footsteps on the Sea* and the success that Parchment had with 'Light Up the

Fire', British Christian music began to develop its own sound and impact.

Bob also helped Key Records gain distribution rights to Larry Norman's *Upon This Rock* album. Geoff Shearn was one of the first to hear it.

> Bob put *Upon This Rock* in my hands. I took it back home and put it on. I could not believe what I was hearing. It was like *Sgt. Pepper's Lonely Hearts Club Band*—the sort of mega transformation that took The Beatles to a whole new plane. I could not believe I was hearing Christian music, it was so good. After Pete and Dave had heard it as well I rushed back to Bob and told him that we had to have it, and so we did our first licensing deal, leasing the album from Benson.
>
> We also started to organise tours bringing over Larry Norman and Randy Stonehill. Larry set a new standard of creativity for us, and he was significant as he was one of the leaders of the Jesus Movement in California and he represented something that was radical, expressive and passionate for Jesus. Of course once we put the album out it became an overnight success.

But there was something else that was happening in the MGO camp. Geoff Shearn's spiritual search was a little different to the other guys', and he was intrigued by worship in a deeper way. So when he was manning the MGO stand in the exhibition area at Spree 73 right next to the Come Together stand, he found himself increasingly drawn to the heart of worship he sensed in the Come Together songs, and he noticed how people at Spree were being drawn to them too.

In fact, at one of the Come Together presentations at All Souls, Langham Place, Geoff Shearn had a conversation with Ian Hamilton and Norman Miller, both executives at Word record company. Ian was unsure of the potential of Come Together, but Geoff was quick to respond. 'Ian, it's a whole new kind of worship that's emerging, it's huge.'

'Do you think this is going to last?' Ian asked.

Geoff replied, 'I think it's the future!'

At the final presentation of Come Together, Geoff heard a song that stopped him in his tracks.

It was at the end of the evening and people sang what felt like a spontaneous song, 'Bind Us Together'. I was absolutely blown away with it and thought it was fantastic. Everybody was arm in arm singing.

I was trying to find out who wrote this song and discovered it was Bob Gillman, from Romford Fellowship. I couldn't believe that he was English. We arranged to meet and I told him it was a fantastic song. He said that it came out of Come Together and that they were all caught up in it, but while it had been great at the time, people had moved on from there. I said that it was a great song but he was dismissive and the whole thing fizzled out a bit.

A year later John Noble, the leader of the Romford Fellowship, said that if I felt we should get some of these homegrown songs out into the mainstream churches, they felt it was part of their responsibility to support me with that. That started the whole development of the worship side of Thankyou Music. In fact, Thankyou Music is now synonymous with worship. There was a wealth of songs that came including songs from Dave Bilbrough and Ian Traynar. Bob Gillman also signed his songs to Thankyou Music.

As Peter Fenwick recalls:

At the time, Romford was really the epicentre of new worship in this country. John and Christine Noble had in their ranks some brilliant creative people, songwriters and artists—Nick Butterworth, for instance, and Mick Inkpen, and they were producing outstanding album, book and magazine artwork, which lifted the whole quality and creativity to another level. From this community came early grassroots recordings with songs from emerging Romford songwriters and spoken word by Christine

Noble and Maurice Smith. John and Christine were 'Mum and Dad', giving room, responsibility and encouragement for these kids to develop. They were producing a community life which was glorious. In my time I've seen a lot of churches and I've not seen one that beats what they had there. I really do believe they were the real pioneers of new worship in this country. This creative community included songwriters Dave Bilbrough, Ian Traynar, Dave Bryant and Bob Gillman, drummer Dave Engel and musical director and producer John Menlove.

John Noble really trusted Geoff Shearn, and observed:

I always felt that Geoff was prophetic. I think he saw something which nobody else at that time was really seeing. He got a hold of it and developed it and made it available. For me Geoff, who was very much in fellowship with us and became a friend, was seeing something. I think sometimes people haven't appreciated just how much of a role he did play in bringing worship the way it is to the UK and beyond. Geoff was an astute and remarkable guy. It wasn't just because he was a business person, because I don't think that was his main gifting. It was that he saw something and persevered with it at the time.

'Bind Us Together' went on to be the first of this new wave of worship songs from the UK church to go around the world and soon became used in many international gatherings. It also became a musical which toured Britain and Scandinavia and featured the songs from the Romford Fellowship.

Another key song in this season was 'Majesty'. In 1977, Jack Hayford and his wife Anna spent their vacation in Great Britain. Jack remembers, 'we travelled through England, Scotland and Wales, the same year that Queen Elizabeth celebrated the twenty-fifth anniversary of her coronation. There were many symbols of royalty all around.' Hayford says the opening lyrics and melody for 'Majesty' came together when he was driving in Great Britain. He completed the song in California, and it went on to become an anthem of worship around the world.

The 1970s ended with two landmark albums. One was Cliff Richard's *Small Corners*, which set a new standard in terms of the quality of UK Christian album releases. The other was Andraé Crouch and the Disciples' *Live in London*. A wonderful recording from Hammersmith and Free Trade Hall in Manchester, capturing contemporary gospel music with many of Andraé's key songs, the album included, 'This Is Another Day', 'My Tribute' and 'Tell Them'. This was the first time UK audiences had seen Andraé. He was one of the rare artists who was embraced by the black church, the white church and the Jesus Movement. Andraé's other key songs were 'The Blood Will Never Lose Its Power', 'Jesus Is the Answer' and 'Soon and Very Soon'. Andraé went on to receive seven Grammy Awards—a true pioneer.

Chapter 3

NEW SHOOTS AND THE EMERGENCE OF KEY INFLUENCERS

Meanwhile, tucked away in a small studio at Elim Bible College in Worcestershire, a gifted German electronics engineer was about to embark on a new adventure. Helmut Kaufmann had come to live in England to train to work with Radio Elwa in Liberia, but had ended up at Bible college, where he developed the campus radio studio into a small recording studio. It was there that he recorded two young songwriters, Ishmael and Andy Piercy, as well as a band called Regeneration. Don Feltham, who then ran Echo Recordings had met Helmut on a radio course and invited him to join the team and fill the vacancy for a technical guy. So in 1972 Helmut, who was 28 years old and not long married to his French wife Elisabeth, moved to Echo Recordings in Eastbourne.

In those days Echo Recordings was mainly involved in producing Christian radio programmes with Dick Saunders and Eric Hutchings. Helmut knew that the setup was basic, but that

Christian music was in short supply. 'So we started recording music ourselves, bringing bands into the Echo studio.'

When a group called Meet Jesus Music came in to record, something changed for Helmut. 'It was one of the major stepping stones to realising what we could do as a Christian studio with an enthusiastic team with skill and determination. It was a tremendous experience recording Meet Jesus Music, and the album got the highest reviews in the Christian music scene when it was released in 1973. For us that was the start of it all.'

The studios were actually built from the old stables of the five-star Grand Hotel, and they continued as a stable and training ground for recording engineers, producers and music makers. Helmut has an amazing gift for identifying potential. Staff recording engineers Andy Kidd, Neil Costello, Dave Aston, Martin Smith, Matthias Kaufmann, Paul Burton, Dave Lynch, Trevor Michael, Phil Johnson, Matt Rowbottom, Mike Newbon and myself all went on to contribute much to Christian music. Many Christian albums were recorded and mixed there, as well as recordings by Paul McCartney, Roger Daltry and Keith Emerson.

The studio's emergence came at just the right time. After the success of Parchment's 'Light Up the Fire' single, John Pantry was inundated with requests to produce new artists and needed a studio. He was introduced to Echo Recordings (which in 1976 changed its name to ICC—International Christian Communications) and began to produce albums from their studio, by artists such as Graham Kendrick, Len Magee, Gwen Murray and The Advocates. One year, John produced sixteen albums. He remembers:

Although at the time ICC's studio was quite basic, I got on so well with Helmut—he has the gift of making everyone feel special—that we ended up agreeing to do some more albums there. It was close to Kingsway and very convenient. I booked into a bed and breakfast place and started doing album after album. I brought all kinds of musicians down to Eastbourne, including some session musicians that I had worked with. These guys were probably pretty amazed, having worked in London studios and other places and then coming to this little place in Eastbourne.

I was enjoying this time on two levels: I was enjoying the fact that I was getting to have a little more artistic freedom—it was a chance to be really creative with the production. I knew that I could take some of the guys who had no experience of professional recording to another level. And I'm sure God used me to do that. On another level for me, spiritually, I was growing all the time. I was meeting some spiritual giants and I was praying with them and they were praying with me and my faith was growing all the time.

Helmut, supported by his wife Elisabeth, sowed so much into countless people over the years—many artists and engineers found their first taste of recording at ICC, where encouragement and help were in plentiful supply. Martin Smith (of Delirious?) credits Helmut as being the 'father of all fathers'.

Through diligence, hard work and prayer, Helmut turned a small, four-track bedroom studio into one of the UK's top recording facilities.

SEVEN KEY INFLUENCERS

At the risk of leaving people off, it is possible to identify a handful of individuals and movements through whom God worked even more powerfully as He nurtured the modern-day worship movement in the UK.

GRAHAM KENDRICK

When Billy Graham spoke at Spree 73, quoting from a song Graham Kendrick had just sung, the young songwriter was surprised. There were many thousands of young people there who had sung songs and hymns written by many people, so to be singled out as one who had captured truth was a real affirmation and encouragement. 'It's a very optimistic time when you are in your early 20s,' Graham explains, 'with a great sense of life being before you. But there was definitely a lot happening, certainly for the people of my age at the time. There was a sense of excitement and of the generation doing it their way.'[1]

Yet Graham's most significant encounter in those days did not happen in an impressive concert venue. It took place in the bathroom.

So there I was in the bathroom when suddenly this strange thing started to happen to me. It felt like I was filling up from the inside, and a big smile appeared on my face! I knelt down in the bath as I began to overflow with a previously unknown experience of joy and the presence of God.

It had a massive impact on my life. The biggest effect was that it introduced me to worship in the Spirit—not that I hadn't been helped by the Spirit before in my worship, but now something tangible was happening inside me. It wasn't just me making up my mind to sing a hymn—it was the Spirit inside, urging me and overflowing with something that I knew didn't come from me. It launched me into a whole process of learning to worship.

I spent a lot of time just shut away in my own room praying, kneeling, standing or raising my hands—learning to worship with my whole being. You name it, I did it! I was getting free of all the inhibitions. I tend to trace much of my worship songwriting back to that time. If you're going to lead people in worship, or write worship songs, you have to be a worshipper. You can't take people where you've never been yourself....

While I was learning the songwriter's and storyteller's craft—which laid the foundation for my worship composing—I was also learning some of the skills for worship leading, the gospel story leading into a heart response.

Through events like Spring Harvest, Youth for Christ tours, and the renewal movement that was affecting most denominations, the culture was changing. Many of us felt that in some way God would visit us and we'd experience his presence in a tangible way. That dynamic was one of the main things that drove the development of what we now call 'worship leading'. There were the beginnings of a sense of adventure—knowing that even if you had your list of songs the worship could veer off in any direction.[2]

A young preacher named Clive Calver with a vision for communicating the message of Jesus in fresh ways gathered a number of talented communicators, including Graham Kendrick, to form a travelling mission team to work alongside local churches. They numbered around ten members and called themselves 'In the Name of Jesus'. 'Church used to mean rubbing shoulders once a week,' Kendrick remembers,

but suddenly through team ministry, our lives were wrapped up in one another. One of the first worship songs I wrote was called 'Jesus Stand Among Us', and the song was an echo of our prayer—'be our sweet agreement at the meeting of our eyes.'

> I wrote a lot of material in response to what was happening in our lives. Somebody would be going through a difficult time and perhaps I'd write a song as my way of trying to encourage them. We were also doing a lot of counselling, so those special moments of prayer and conversation are probably reflected in songs over the years.

The song 'Jesus Stand Among Us' would become the title track for Graham's first album of worship songs.

> At that time, there was very little publishing infrastructure for new praise and worship songs, and songs spread by word of mouth. During a meeting, people would copy the words from the overhead projector and guess the chords as we played. Geoff Shearn was working for Kingsway Music, who were just beginning to publish *Songs of Fellowship*. In the late 70s Geoff discovered that I had a stockpile of worship songs I had written, so it was suggested that I record some of them. I dug them out of a drawer and started releasing worship albums alongside the more performance material.

This was not something Graham had jumped at immediately.

> I saw myself as a performing artist, and I remember resisting the suggestion of leading worship at the first

ever Spring Harvest in 1979. I saw myself singing to people—not leading them in singing. Becoming a worship leader felt almost like I'd come to an end of something, and I have to confess that I saw the role of worship leader as somewhat second class.

But increasingly I realised that God was doing something new in the area of worship and many of the skills I'd learned in performing enabled me to serve what was happening. When I finally stopped the concert work [in the early 80s] I suddenly felt liberated. My wife, Jill, said it was like a burden had lifted from me and I was doing exactly what I should do, as I was so much freer.

Spring Harvest created a platform and demand for new songs. A whole generation was expressing itself differently and doing church differently. A new era had begun for me, as well as [for] the church.[3]

Geoff Shearn knew Graham well, and could see the ways in which God was using him. 'Because he himself had come from a non-charismatic background, he was able to grow up with the audience and gradually lead them into a richer worship experience.' Graham was also able to carry over his gift of poetic and powerful pictures in his lyrics to his worship songs.

Matt Redman's opinion is equally positive: 'Every song I've ever seen of Graham's seems to be crammed full of poetic, divine, biblical truth. These songs have travelled all around the world ushering in the revelation of God to thousands of hearts.'

Martin Smith also holds fond memories:

> I was twelve when I walked into the big top
> at Spring Harvest for the very first time, I can
> still remember the feeling of electricity passing
> through my body as I heard this music belting
> out from the stage, and hearing 5,000 people
> singing their hearts out. 'Shine, Jesus, Shine' was
> the anthem the saints were singing, and that was
> the moment the church in Britain went from feel-
> ing small to thinking big. Who was this guy who
> spoke with such authority and churned out all
> these amazing anthems? I knew at that moment
> that this is what I wanted to do with my life.[4]

DAVE BILBROUGH

Church leader Peter Fenwick first met Dave Bilbrough at the
Cauliflower Pub in Romford. It was a Saturday night; Peter was
preaching and Dave was leading worship. 'It was Dave's first
big outing. He was seventeen or eighteen at the most, and the
worship was terrific. I realised that not only was he very good
at the job of worship leading, he was a lovely guy and a man of
integrity.'

Dave was not from a Christian background but had started
going along to church when he was sixteen. Dave remembers,
'Although I couldn't doubt the sincerity of much of the worship,
the terms, phrases and all the way that things were put across

weren't from a culture that I was from. I asked my dad for a guitar and started to play purely to express what I'd found in God, which was very real to me.'

Dave's musical style, more influenced by Paul Simon and Bob Dylan than by Charles Wesley and Ira D Sankey, connected well with a youth group he was part of that begun to meet together.

> There had been about forty or fifty of us young people [who had left the traditional church and started meeting] and we had started to call ourselves some sort of church, but we really didn't know much at all. We were quite innocent when it came to knowing how to structure a church. A friendship was formed initially between Nick Butterworth and John Noble, which subsequently resulted in John becoming influential in our situation by way of his experience and gifting. At the time, John was just beginning to lead weekly meetings with Maurice Smith on Saturday evenings at the Cauliflower Pub.
>
> Those meetings were very charismatic and Holy Spirit orientated. They would take the shape of people sitting in a round as opposed to a platform-type meeting. It wasn't terribly structured. Looking back there were probably some great meetings and some really naff ones, as there always are, but there was a real sense of the presence of the Holy Spirit. It was very dynamic and

fresh and spontaneous and people were speaking of God in very personal terms, as opposed to the tradition we'd come to know before. There was a sense of community beginning to be established.

John was very much the apostolic figure—getting people together and shaping up groups. We saw him as a father figure and overseer of our group. John helped nurture our sense that worship was going to be the way forward, and that it wasn't going to be accomplished by doing [church the way it had been done up till now]. They gave space to me and to a number of others. Were it not for their encouragement, where would I be? I'm eternally grateful for that.

Nick Butterworth was a creative leader, mentor and provoker to Dave. Influenced by L'Abri and the teaching of Francis Schaeffer, Nick encouraged high standards of creativity and believed that creative expression was more than a means to an end but that the church was called to be a community expressing its values through creativity. Dave notes how groundbreaking it was to see these artistic insights infiltrate into the arena of Spirit-led worship.

Out of that sense of community came songs which expressed what the speakers were saying, including Dave's song 'Abba, Father', which was written at a difficult time in his life.

'If you look at church history, you'll find this was often the case,' he explains. 'The songwriters recorded what the theme and focus of church was at the time. Songs like "Jesus, Take Me as I

Am", "Bind Us Together" and "Abba, Father", came out of the focus of what people were saying in those days.'

Like so many other worship leaders, Dave was impacted by Come Together. 'We got behind it as a choir and group of musicians and ourselves, and toured around the London area with it,' he recalls. 'That was a catalyst for lots of things because it brought together a unified group of musicians on a bigger scale, and with the Albert Hall meetings as well, people were beginning to move in a bigger arena.'

In his troubadour style, Dave would go on to write many well-loved songs, including 'All Hail the Lamb', 'I Am a New Creation' and 'Army of Ordinary People'.

Wayne Drain, Pastor of Fellowship of Christians Church in Russellville, Arkansas comments, 'I think Dave Bilbrough is a remarkable statesman, a humble guy. In some ways he was like the Matt Redman of his generation. Dave was the first British musician to come to our church, and I remember that people went away from our church saying: that guy has got great songs, but did you hear what he said about relationship?'

Dave has always been an ambassador of diversity. Recording engineer and producer Neil Costello remembers 'I worked on four or five albums with Dave Bilbrough. There was a lot of soft rock sound happening then and Dave was quite keen to try other things such as mandolins and accordions, and perhaps go with a more Cajun sound. I think what he brought into the sound of worship was don't just go down the one route: be open to other musical styles.' This was enforced further by prophet Dale Gentry, who spoke over Dave about bringing new rhythms and new sounds, as he has continued to do.

CHRIS BOWATER

Chris Bowater came from a Pentecostal background, grew up in Birmingham and attended the Royal College of Music in London where he trained with the orchestral conductor Adrian Boult. After college, Chris got married and raised his family in Lincoln. It was there that he became involved in coordinating the local performance of Come Together. He formed a choir called the New Life Singers that brought people from local Methodist, Baptist and Anglican churches together with those in the Assemblies of God church where he worshipped.

After Come Together, Jimmy and Carol Owens wrote two more musicals, If My People and The Witness, and Chris was involved in the UK presentations. He then wrote and recorded his own musical called Miracle followed by the recording of the *Maranatha—Second Coming* album. Chris also began to develop a worship training programme in the church.

> We did a worship school which ran for seventeen years, that was all part of the process of touching a lot of lives around the country, and some of our contacts overseas. I was introduced to Stuart Bell, who was pastoring an independent charismatic church. Stuart had been part of a band called The Advocates. In many ways he'd been part of pioneering Christian music, playing at the Royal Albert Hall and the Festival of Light.

Stuart and I developed our identity and came out of the Assemblies of God in order to facilitate a vision that was happening in the area called 'Grapevine'. Grapevine and the Ground Level churches developed and emerged. The Grapevine Bible Week was held for over thirty years—one of the longest running Bible weeks in this country.

I have been the Director of Music for all of that time. What we have tried to do is to develop what we call team worship leading, rather than the single worship leader. We facilitate each meeting with three worship leaders working together.

Chris is a prolific songwriter, yet one of his songs—'Jesus, Your Love Has Melted My Heart'—was tagged 'author unknown' when it was first published. It was a popular song, but for a number of years many were unaware that Chris had written it. Chris Head of Springtide Publishing Company—who wrote and produced the groundbreaking Kingsway-released album *Valley of Achor*—was determined to discover its origin. It took a bit of digging, but eventually the trail led him to Chris Bowater. When Chris Head phoned to ask if he was the writer of the song, Chris Bowater told him that he was. 'He asked if I'd written any others. I said "Yes, a few hundred". This was how it was in that season; I was writing morning, noon and night.'

It wasn't just the songwriting that Chris threw himself into. He pushed musical boundaries too, as Pentecostal churches became some of the first in the UK to have drums. 'We'd often have more instruments. It was conventional to have the piano and Hammond organ but there were often other instruments in the mix too. It was a very musical environment.' This encouraged Chris in his leading of worship from the keyboard, where he was also influenced by Andraé Crouch, Ken Medema and Keith Green.

Chris Bowater is like King David—a man after God's own heart. He is well loved and hugely respected. Chris has been a pastor to many musicians, and as a worship leader he is very sensitive to following the scent of the Holy Spirit. Chris has a real desire for the nations, especially France, and has ministered in Asia several times.

His album *Time for Tears* really captured his heart and followed on from the classic recording *Highest Honour*, which included 'Jesus Will Take the Highest Honour'.

Chris has a heart to teach and train others and founded the School of Creative Ministries which has been running for over twenty years. This has seen hundreds of worship leaders and musicians equipped to serve in their local churches. Chris also developed the Worship Academy which has been held in Singapore, Thailand, Portugal, South Africa, France, Romania and the USA.

NOEL RICHARDS

Born in South Wales, Noel first saw Graham Kendrick perform at Bristol's Colston Hall on the It's Buzz tour, organised by MGO to promote *Buzz* magazine, in 1971. He knew right away that he wanted to follow Graham's lead. Over the course of the next few years, Noel spent all of his free time playing coffee bars and evangelistic events in and around South Wales. In October 1975, after an introduction to Avon Youth for Christ (YFC), through his pastor John Glass (later Secretary General of the Elim Pentecostal Churches), Noel joined YFC, playing in a band called Seed. Seed quickly became popular, and when Clive Calver became YFC's UK director (with Graham Kendrick the musical director), Seed played at Clive's induction.

Noel worked as a YFC associate between 1975 and 1979, gaining valuable experience in the recording studio and as a singer/songwriter. Noel married Tricia in 1978 and in the autumn of that year, met Gerald Coates for the first time, when he visited their church in Plymouth. Over the next eighteen months Gerald visited the church frequently. In early 1980, the church closed down and Noel and Tricia, along with a group of more than fifty others moved to Cobham, Surrey, to be a part of Cobham Christian Fellowship. Noel began to lead worship at the church and also performed several nights each week in a number of local wine bars.

At the start of 1983, Noel left his regular daytime job and began what would be many years travelling with Gerald Coates, who considers him a man of integrity. 'I've seen Noel in tears over the burdens that God has put on his heart,' Gerald says. 'He would travel with me and drive, while I was dictating mail and stuff. He would sing a song or two in the meetings, not usually worship songs, although he'd written one or two good ones by then, including "Lord and Father, King Forever." And then he and Tricia wrote the classic, "All Heaven Declares."'

John Noble also saw Noel's strengths, such as 'his faithfulness in doing what God has led him to do. His boldness to do what he does, but without any self-praise; he just gets on and does it. He's never been affected by his acceptance and fame if you like. He's always encouraged others.'

Clive Calver came to see Noel as 'one of the understated heroes.'

> The ebullient militancy that comes through with 'He Is Risen' and some of his other songs is terrific. The way he and Trish work together with some of the gentle love songs to Jesus, and the way they can also burst eardrums when they really get going—Noel did an incredible amount to make worship exciting, and it was very hard to worship quietly and passively [when he was leading]. Noel had this wonderful fun about him and this sense of really wanting the people of God to be excited about what they had.

Noel signed with Kingsway Music, and in 1990 released the popular recording *By Your Side*, which included 'There Is Power in the Name of Jesus', 'You Laid Aside Your Majesty', and 'Our Confidence (He Is Our Fortress)'. This was followed in 1993 with *Thunder in the Skies* which included 'To Be in Your Presence' and 'Great Is the Darkness (Come Lord Jesus)'. The album was well received, especially by UK Christian bookshop owners, and they voted it Album of the Year in 1994. These and Noel's other recordings have always included a combination of self-written songs and songs from other writers, including Doug Horley's 'We Want to See Jesus Lifted High'. Noel was a generous gatherer.

Beth Redman remembers:

> When I was very young I saw a song on the
> overhead was written by a married couple and
> something about that really impacted me. I loved
> worship and worshipping was the highlight for
> me at our church. We sang a lot of songs from
> Downs Bible Week and worship music was
> played a lot in my house.
>
> One Sunday we sang a song written by Noel
> and Tricia Richards, even as a young child I knew
> God was speaking to me that one day I would do
> that with my husband too. A huge concept for a
> small child but I truly believed it was from God.

Beth and her husband Matt would go on to write many classic
songs for the church including 'Blessed Be Your Name' and 'You
Never Let Go'.

ISHMAEL

Thanks to the encouragement of Phil Vogel—who was the
National Director of Youth for Christ and a father figure to many,
including fellow songwriters Andy Piercy and Noel Richards—a
young man named Ian Smale took his first steps into the world
of worship and evangelism in 1970.

'When I became a Christian', he says, 'I found church services very difficult because they were very, very traditional. The

bit I liked best was the Bible teaching, but the music … I just didn't relate to it at all. So right from the word go I felt the music needed to change if we were going to reach different people.'

Ishmael started to write songs with his friend Andy Piercy, who felt the same way about worship in church. Their non-religious freedom was as refreshing as it was raw, and soon British Youth for Christ took Ishmael and Andy on board as associate evangelists.

Working with Andy Piercy and adopting the name Ishmael (which Phil Vogel had nicknamed him when he was eleven), he wrote evangelistic praise songs with a purpose, and a sense of humour.

> We were there to shake up the traditions. When people got too serious with their music we would talk about how we just wanted to present God to people. Whether it was Christians or those not yet Christians, it was all done in a humorous way.
>
> There was an album I brought out called *The Charge of the Light Brigade*, which brought me such a lot of trouble because it was the first time somebody had actually brought tongue-in-cheek humour into Christian music.

For Andy Piercy, it was a unique opportunity.

> Ishmael is a master of 'the three chord trick'[5] and he loves a tune which gets inside your head. Kids

love it and it is foot-stomping, acoustic rock stuff
sharing about the exuberance of knowing Christ.
I don't think that anybody was doing anything
remotely like that back in 1973 and 1974. Most
of the Christian bands were doing [the British
folk music classic] 'Streets of London' and everything was just very serious, which was all right at
the time. Ishmael brought something different;
the exhilaration of exuberant praise. It took a lot
of time for some people to catch on to what he
was doing, but when they did they discovered a
new freedom in praise.

At the time, there was great excitement in the church as the
Redemption Hymnal was released. For Ishmael, who started as a
Baptist and by this time had become an Elim pastor, the changes
in the way the church worshipped were exciting. 'They were like
pub songs. I loved the fact that at last happy music had come
into the church. I do believe it was a great help in releasing joy
in praise. But you've got to bear in mind that the vast majority of
Pentecostals who sang these lively "clap along" hymns were very,
very serious people. I upset a few of them because they didn't think
they were fun songs! Even so I'd still shake the songs about a bit.'

Ishmael went on to form Ishmael United, invent the 'Glories'
concept albums for children, pioneer the idea of family worship,
and start Praise Parties at Spring Harvest. He also wrote dozens of
simple Scripture memory songs as well as eventually writing the
classic song 'Father God, I Wonder'.

Ishmael was also a leader in the Arun Fellowship, where Cutting Edge/Delirious? were based. Keyboard player Tim Jupp, and drummer Stew Smith would tour with Ishmael and work on many of his albums, as well as be part of Praise Parties. Pat Bilbrough, with her expertise with children's choirs, would also work on Ishmael's recordings.

Ishmael brought two things to worship that were absolutely critical; sound scripture and a theology of spiritual warfare. Both of these he introduced in ways that touched the hearts of children.

However, Ishmael found that focusing on children labelled him and meant that he was no longer considered an adult worship leader.

> People could not accept that I enjoyed doing both, I think they thought what I did was too simplistic for adults, which I found very sad. I believe a true worship leader should be able to communicate and encourage worship in all ages even if their main gifting is with a specific age group.
>
> I do believe we have missed out on the whole family concept of praise and worship together. There must be a place where the church meets together and that all ages praise God together. With all styles of music, my heart is that every week we're doing something for all ages that children enjoy, even if it's just in part of our service. I believe God loves seeing His family having fun and worshipping all together.

DAVE FELLINGHAM

Dave Fellingham's roots were in the Salvation Army, where from a very young age he understood the place of music in evangelism. He was also stirred by the content of the experience and holiness songs of Wesley and the Booths. The heartfelt experiential worship of his childhood and teens became a long-lasting influence.

Like Ishmael and Noel Richards, Dave Fellingham attended an Elim church for a time. Unlike his fellow worship leaders, Dave's journey involved a detour.

> Spiritually my life went a bit off course for a while, mainly because my wife and I couldn't really settle in a church near our home in Brighton. We weren't happy in any of the churches we tried and it made me a bit rootless. I got very heavily involved in any kind of secular music and was trying to make it as a composer and conductor. It became a bit of a diversion really.
>
> But in 1973 there was an event in Brighton called Faith Outreach, which was produced on the back of the Festival of Light. Because of my musical background I was asked by the committee if I would organise all the music. I agreed, put a band together and it was then that I met Ian Barclay, the new vicar at St Luke's. He rescued me out of my spiritual doldrums and was very encouraging, and my wife and I started going to his church.

The mid-week meeting was charismatic and open to the gifts of the Spirit. Over the next couple of years the church evolved and eventually I went full-time with the mandate to help the church in worship and to train leaders. David and Dale Garratt were just beginning to write the Scripture in Song songs, and I thought, 'I could do that', and I did. Not for any ambitious reason, but we were constantly looking for new songs to sing. I wrote one called 'Hallelujah! The Lord Reigns' and taught it to the church at St Luke's and it became a song we sang on Sundays as well as mid-week. It was the first of many songs with counterpoint melodies that I wrote in those days. Barney Coombs then picked it up and taught it to the Basingstoke Community Church, where David and Dale Garratt visited, heard the song and published it.

In time, Terry Virgo moved from Seaford to Brighton, and Dave joined his leadership team, alongside a man named Henry Tyler, leading the new church in Clarendon Villas, Hove.

Terry was the apostolic figure and the prophetic go-getter, I was the young guy coming through and Henry was the father of it all who'd been around for years and years. He came out of a strong reformed position, strong on preaching the Word, but was also a very lively man in the

Holy Spirit and a lot of fun to be with. He had
an incredible knowledge of hymns and always
encouraged us with the new wave of worship
to not forget our hymnology. He loved the new
songs, though, and he even wrote one, 'Rejoice
in the Lord Always'! He kept hymns alive in the
midst of the new songs coming through.

It was Henry who gave me a love of the theology of worship. He put a lot into me in my
early years and I've never lost it. I would love to
see it rediscovered more by contemporary worship leaders and songwriters.

Dave went on to become the key worship leader at Downs
Bible Week, one of the largest and most influential gatherings of
the church calendar, but it was the foundations laid in these early
years that really shaped him.

Dave's songs are always full of Biblical truth and substance,
such as 'God of Glory', 'At Your Feet We Fall', and 'Shout for Joy
and Sing'. Journalist Dave Roberts wrote, 'If Graham Kendrick
is the modern-day Wesley, then Dave Fellingham is the modern
day Watts'.[6] Terry Virgo says, 'I think Dave Fellingham has been a
wonderful father figure to a number of young musicians, and has
been outstanding in giving them space, encouraging them through
and helping them hone their gift. Dave has created a context of
mutual encouragement and honouring one another.'

Dave has been the spiritual father to a 'creative community'
in Brighton, working with gifted worship leaders and musicians

including Stuart Townend, Kate Simmonds, Paul Oakley, Lou Fellingham, Phatfish, Simon Brading and Sam Cox, as well as Mark Edwards and Raul D'Oliveira. Dave has also written the excellent book *Worship Restored*.

In a *Cross Rhythms* article in 1990, James Attlee wrote of Dave: 'He is rightly tagged a Renaissance Man, but the renaissance he is involved in does not look back for its inspiration to the art and philosophy of the classical world. Instead, Dave and people like him have rediscovered the Biblical mandate for artistic expression and in so doing, hope to trigger an explosion of creativity that will extend beyond the boundaries of the church, and make a real and positive contribution to twentieth century culture.'[7]

Worship leader Fred Heumann says,

> The role Dave has had in establishing an environment where people were affirmed musically, trained biblically and released spiritually has made all the difference in the world. Whenever I am teaching about being a pastor to musicians and nurturing them, I speak about Dave. I know his heart for and commitment to biblical worship and excellent musicianship, and his refusal to compromise on things of the Spirit. Dave has modelled something that we only dream of— being a pastor to musicians and calling them to a high biblical standard. Dave's a musician but he's also a pastor and a preacher and there's a model there for people.

BRYN HAWORTH

Bryn is a master musician, an excellent slide guitarist, and a mentor to many. He was one of the first very gifted musicians to become a lead worshipper. Bryn was raised in the Lancashire town of Darwen, and in 1973 he and his wife Sally gave their lives to God in a tent crusade. Signed with secular companies Island and A&M Records, Bryn recorded the classic albums *Let the Days Go By* (1974), *Sunny Side of the Street* (1975), *Grand Arrival* (1978), and *Keep the Ball Rolling* (1979), worked with mainstream artists Cliff Richard, Joan Armatrading, Gerry Rafferty and Fairport Convention, and also appeared on the Old Grey Whistle Test. Bryn's own solo recordings have been milestones in the evolution of Christian music. Bryn is a sanctified blues man and a sensitive worship leader, a renowned virtuoso on the guitar.

Bryn and Sally lived in California for a while, and visited the first Vineyard church in Los Angeles, pastored by Ken Gulliksen, where Bryn really connected with God through the worship, and brought the songs back to his local church. Bryn and Sally became two of the founding members of Vineyard UK, and Bryn led worship at many of the Vineyard UK conferences, as well as New Wine.

Stuart Townend, who would later play keyboards for Bryn, says, 'Bryn's thing was space and not pushing it. His worship leading was in some ways anonymous and there was always a value to the music. There was that sense of just being able to wait on the Lord. Bryn also brought a musical excellence that sharpened you up.'

A memorable time was at the end of his set at an event called Banquet, held at Wembley Arena. Bryn went into 'He is Lord', taking it from performance into worship, which was unique at this time. Other memorable recordings include Bryn leading 'More Love, More Power' at Spring Harvest on the 1987 live album.

When Bryn recorded an album in the Worship Leader series called *More Than a Singer* for Kingsway in 1992, *Cross Rhythms* magazine reviewed it saying, 'As a signpost of where praise and worship can go in the 90s this is a milestone album'.[8]

Bryn has recorded many classic albums, including three on the Chapel Lane label (*The Gap, Pass It On, Wings of the Morning*), as well as *Mountain Mover, Blue and Gold, Live, Slide Don't Fret, Songs and Hymns, Time Out* and *Rebel Man*. These albums are full of faith-building songs and skilful musicianship. Bryn's eighteen albums recorded over four decades have contained some of the highlights of post-war Christian music.

Bryn also featured on the Vineyard album *Take Our Lives* and recorded the *Finer Things* project with Kevin Prosch. Kevin became a good friend, visiting Bryn and Sally at home. He remembers:

> I would go and spend the night with them and we would bring out the instruments and we didn't have to talk. We said everything we wanted to say after we finished playing. That's very powerful. As far as impact goes, I was just surprised, Bryn was the first person I'd met who was a believer and knew that there was such a thing as a baritone or mandocello or any of those kind of things. Before

you just didn't talk about it that much as there
wasn't anyone around who knew about it. Bryn not
only knew what they were but had some of them
and played them; this was an inspiration to me.

In 1990, when Bryn and Sally came onto staff at South West
London Vineyard church, their pastor said his first task was to get
the music up and running in church, then he would start a prison
ministry. The church has faithfully persevered with this and now
has an effective prison ministry.

God has used Bryn to inspire many gifted musicians in the
church to take their place in the worship teams and play their part,
stepping up to their priestly call to care passionately about the
praise of God.

Bryn was just one of a new wave of excellent musicians bringing their skills to the world of worship. As He did with Graham
Kendrick, God was changing the hearts of many musicians as he
revealed the importance of worship, not just performance.

Previously, the UK Contemporary Christian Music (CCM)
scene had been vibrant, but with a low regard for the worship of the
church. This was left to the less skilful musicians. As worship was
restored, CCM became more worshipful, and the worship became
more creative. Laurie Mellor observes that 'in the 1980s, more
and more musicians who had been involved in bands were leading
worship at church. The musical standards of people involved in
leading worship improved.'[9]

For several years the UK church came together to worship
and pray at the NEC in Birmingham. These Prayer For Revival

events also provided a platform for the leading musicians (Levites) to be part of the worship team, fulfilling their calling to be not just players, but priests.

We have touched on just a few here, but the list of names we could have included was extensive: Raul D'Oliveira, Terl Bryant, Neil Costello, David and Carrie Grant, Andy Piercy, Martin Neil, Dave Markee, Phil Crabbe, Dave Clifton, Brian Houston, Nicky Brown, John Perry, Dave Fitzgerald, Steve Gregory, Mark Edwards and many more.

Chapter 4

FESTIVALS AND STREAMS

Alongside the new musicians coming up, and/or moving from performance into worship leading, there were new events and moves of God shaping the worship story at this time.

GREENBELT

The year 1974 saw the first Greenbelt festival, a Christian Arts festival held in a field in East Anglia, which grew to become a significant event.

Well into the 1990s Greenbelt was the main UK festival you attended to hear an amazing collection of artists and bands from around the world, as well as many key teachers and influencers such as Larry Norman, Randy Stonehill, John Smith, Tony Campolo, Mike Yaconelli, Graham Cray and Jim Wallis. Headline performers included artists as varied as Cliff Richard, After the Fire, Deniece Williams, Steve Taylor, Philip Bailey, Koinonia, Charlie Peacock and Ladysmith Black Mambazo.

The seminars always had a strong emphasis on justice, under-standing culture and taking our place as creative people in it, and still do; recent speakers have included Martin Wroe and Cole Moreton.

1979 was a landmark year when After the Fire (led by Andy Piercy and Pete Banks), who were making a major impact in the mainstream, performed, Larry Norman, Randy Stonehill and Bryn Haworth took part and Cliff Richard headlined, on the same weekend his single 'We Don't Talk Anymore' went to number one in the mainstream British charts.

Two years later the festival 'had a surprise set', to quote Stewart Henderson.[1]

There was something touching in the phone call received by the Greenbelt on-site office over the bank holiday weekend of 1981. It was U2, who were ringing up to see if they could come and play a short set at the festival. Borrowing amps and a drum kit from the weekend's other acts, they lashed out twenty minutes of musical power and lyrical depth. Within two years they would become a major force in British music, with a number one album, *War*, before going on to become the most popular rock band in the world.

Greenbelt has played a major role in encouraging Christians to take their place in society and set a high standard in terms of big scale events.

Always tinged with a challenge for musicians to get out of the Christian ghetto, the festival has played a key role in breaking down the wall between the sacred and the secular.

At its best, Greenbelt remains singular in its faith-affirming, politically engaged, life-transforming experience. As the Canadian singer Bruce Cockburn put it, 'the festival and the people involved in it are the closest thing I have to church. There is a sense of community built around a worshipful intent and a shared understanding of the need to question in the context of faith.'[2]

John Bell and the Iona Community have been a major influence in the worship at Greenbelt combined with the songs of worship and justice from pioneer Garth Hewitt. The key songs from John Bell have included 'Jesus Christ Is Waiting' and 'Touching Place'.

THE ANGLICAN RENEWAL

At the International Renewal Conference organised by Michael Harper and his Fountain Trust in Guildford Cathedral in 1971, David Watson, leader of St Michael Le Belfrey, York, met Merv and Merla Watson from Canada. He commented that they were able to convey a wonderful sense of the Lord and make us deeply aware of His glory and grace.

David invited them to two festivals of praise in York, at which they were joined by a large team of singers and dancers. Then, in 1973, they went with him on a seven-week tour of New Zealand. David commented, 'I have never before in missions worked with

singers of the style of Merv and Merla, but have become increasingly convinced of the power of praise, and I look forward to
combining this with the more conventional proclamation of the
gospel.'[3] It was a bold and enlightened step which was to revolutionise his work as an evangelist.

David began to work with worship ministry The Fisherfolk,
from the Church of the Redeemer, Houston. The Fisherfolk came
to Britain in 1973 with the Rev Graham Pulkingham, and led
many festivals of praise in cathedrals around the country. David
would often give the closing address, and he found that their
worship created just the right atmosphere for the subsequent proclamation of God's word. The Fisherfolk broke the mould creatively
and modelled flowing in the Spirit in worship.

David soon recognised the need for a team to travel with him
wherever he was invited to go, leading the worship and illumi-
nating his message with drama and dance. In this he was able to
harness the considerable talent of St Michael Le Belfrey's Andrew
Maries, who had gathered around him a band of skilled instru-
mentalists and singers, some of whom would travel with David.
Whenever David was leading at a festival or mission he would take
his own team to lead worship.

Graham Cray remembers:

> After Merv and Merla, The Fisherfolk were pro-
> foundly influential on St Michael Le Belfrey. Their
> vision for worship took root in The Belfrey, and
> David and Ann Watson were thrilled with it. I
> think the first stage of the renewal was individuals

being empowered by the Spirit for witness and the ministry of the gifts. In came a whole new burst of creativity. The Belfrey had become the place! It had become the Holy Trinity Brompton (HTB) or St Andrew's Chorleywood of its time. People came from all over the country and all over the world to ask 'how do you do it?' We would then run conferences and have over 100 leaders live with us for a week. I wanted to see an environment in every church that was open to the Spirit of God, that allowed God to stir up creativity and that served those people to make the best of it.

Before the services at The Belfrey the singers and dancers and drama guys would worship the Lord on the streets. The worship, the drama, the mime, it was all the expression of the creativity of the Spirit of God and the family of God, the body of Christ. It became the most profoundly attractive evangelistic thing!

We were definitely not singing rock music of any sort in those early meetings but there were new songs, so although the wine skin was only a bit more relaxed than organs, hymns and choirs, the lyrics carried the message of the new wine. We didn't have a lot of contact with the house churches and that whole stream. There was no feeling of hostility, I just think the streams ran parallel for a while.

Mike Pilavachi, youth pastor at St Andrew's Chorleywood, comments that the worship from the Anglican stream was very folky and sung with slightly operatic voices. 'This was great for a season but did not compare to the new songs I'd been hearing coming from Dave Bilbrough and Graham Kendrick. They had a vibe musically, as well as a sense of anointing that was missing from our stuff.'

Graham Kendrick moved in 1979 to be part of St Michael Le Belfrey. He remembers:

> The Belfrey was a very innovative centre with a lot of dance, drama and music. They were pioneers in the Anglican Renewal movement, yet still had a bedrock of tradition. That gave me more of an appreciation of liturgy, which began to surface in my songwriting. When I started to write Praise Marches some described them as liturgy on the streets.
>
> I actually wrote 'Servant King' there as a theme song for Spring Harvest 1984, and it contains the line; 'Hands that flung stars into space to cruel nails surrendered'. I can remember composing it in my little music room at our house in York. I wrote it on the piano—despite my severe limitations on that instrument. My colleague Chris Norton helped me make the piano part more presentable.

It was an inspiring time.

Another strand of Anglican Renewal was the worship team Cloud, inspired by The Fisherfolk. Formed in 1972, and led by Phil

Lawson-Johnson, Cloud started off at a place called The Kitchen, near Gloucester Road in south-west London. They recorded their first album in 1974, in St Paul's, Onslow Square, a church they then became part of and started leading worship at once a month. This was radical in terms of the introduction of contemporary worship to HTB, as in 1976, St Paul's merged with HTB, and a new evening service was started. That service was the real growth point of the church, and became bigger than the morning service. Cloud led the worship there for twelve years, with Phil leading the team until 1988. Cloud went on to record seven albums. As Andy Piercy remembers 'Cloud helped create an environment and worship culture at HTB which lay the foundations deep and strong, preparing the ground for a move of the Holy Spirit. They were hugely influential and knew how to flow with the Holy Spirit. Phil Lawson-Johnson's song "We Will Magnify" became popular across the UK church.'

As Graham Cray noted, above, the Anglican Renewal and house church movement were on parallel tracks. It was John Wimber who brought them together, as Phil Lawson-Johnson explains:

> The Fountain Trust had had a big impact for the Anglicans, but when that finished in 1980 there was a bit of a vacuum. When John Wimber arrived he brought people together. I remember Sandy Millar [HTB], Roger Forster [Icthus], Gerald Coates [Pioneer], Terry Virgo [Newfrontiers] and Colin Dye [Kensington Temple] all attending the Vineyard gathering at the Royal Albert Hall. This

made a statement that we were all together. It was
very powerful. John Wimber was a catalyst for
that, undoubtedly.

The third strand in the Anglican Renewal was Prom Praise under
the leadership of Noel Tredinnick. Taking the model of the BBC
Proms—a season of orchestral celebrations—Prom Praise started in
November 1977 with the All Souls Orchestra and choir. Its first ever
concert was held in All Souls, Langham Place, London. Brahms and
Wesley, Bach and Kendrick, were performed side by side in a unique
musical combination—a powerful symphonic sound—bringing a
much-welcomed classical colour to praise and worship. The concert
has been held annually ever since, moving out to the Barbican Hall in
November 1985, then to the Royal Albert Hall in February 1988. The
orchestra and choir have also toured to other cities and have recorded
with Cliff Richard and many distinguished guests.

Prom Praise is an extravagant expression of worship with a full
symphony orchestra, a 300-piece choir, and the Royal Albert Hall
organ. This is a real taste of the tabernacle!

BRITISH BLACK GOSPEL

In 1979, both Maxine and the Majestic Singers and Kainos
stepped onto the scene, recording albums at ICC Studios. This
reflected the creativity coming from the growing number of black
majority churches in the UK. The pioneering recordings were
greatly inspired by Andraé Crouch. Paradise, with lead singer
Doug Williams, were popular at Greenbelt and played support to

Andraé Crouch on his tour of the UK, and also recorded important albums on the Ebony record label, part of Pilgrim Records.

Bazil Meade, ex-keyboard player for Kainos, who is now credited as the godfather of British gospel music, was in conversation with Lawrence Johnson (Church of the Latter Rain Outpouring Revival), John Francis (the Inspirational Choir) and Delroy Powell (New Testament Assembly Choir) and the idea was born that they should arrange a concert for their united choirs. 'We thought it would be a celebration of singing and a training opportunity. If it went well, we thought maybe we could repeat it the following year.'

Rehearsals for the event went extremely well and it was decided to name the choir the London Community Gospel Choir. The first official concert was held at Kensington Temple in May 1983.

LCGC, as it is now known, became an effective training ground for gifted singers and musicians to develop. The choir has sung on albums with Paul McCartney, and in live concerts with Diana Ross and Stevie Wonder. Viv Broughton, owner of the Premises recording and rehearsal studios, said 'Nobody has contributed more to gospel music in Britain over the past thirty years than Bazil Meade. Bazil had the vision to cross denominational boundaries and create a great community choir for London.' Worship leader Mark Beswick remembers 'I was drawn to LCGC by the vision of a united church. LCGC provided the platform for many of us who didn't subscribe to the doctrinal prejudices of the previous generation and future generations to follow.'[4]

Television programmes *People Get Ready* (Channel 4) and *Rock Gospel* (BBC One) helped lift the profile of British gospel music, while LCGC began to travel beyond Britain.

Steve Thompson, keyboard player for the Majestic Singers, and Noel Robinson had also become part of Graham Kendrick's team and Noel and Steve's influence increased with Steve becoming Graham's musical director and record producer.

Although most gospel choirs and artists were covering American recordings, or re-arranging traditional hymns, it was soon time for them to write their own songs. As Mark Beswick remembers:

> It was the late 1980s. I was a member of LCGC and had travelled with the choir on one of their tours to Scandinavia. I don't recall exactly where we were, but it was an outdoor festival of some kind and we were one of the artists on the bill.
>
> It was a hot day and we were due to go on much later in the programme, so we had an opportunity to mill around and listen to the other artists who were performing. I remember standing in the middle of the crowd of people who had gathered around the stage to listen, and a man with an acoustic guitar started to play and sing his songs. The crowd seemed to know them and sang along, and as I listened, I felt the presence of God and I knew in that moment that what I was witnessing was something significant.
>
> As a choir, LCGC had travelled extensively throughout the UK and Europe and I had seen the expression of joy and peace on the faces of hundreds of people, and had even seen a number

of people healed and set free by the power of God. But there was something about this moment in the middle of a field in a foreign land that spoke to my heart. I turned to Bazil Meade, our choir leader, who was standing beside me at the time, and said, 'Bazil, I think this is what we're supposed to be doing.' Bazil smiled and nodded, and we continued to listen to the man with his guitar, singing out his God songs.

I later discovered that man's name was Graham Kendrick. It would be some years before I became a worship leader in my own right, but I believe the seed of worship was sown in my heart in a field by a man with a guitar singing out his love songs to Father God.

When he did become a worship leader, Mark joined forces with Howard Francis, who had been writing songs for the choir including their first single, 'Fill My Cup', and playing keyboard on Noel Richards' albums and several other Kingsway albums. Mark and Howard were an excellent combination, and went on to form Power Praise, writing many wonderful new worship songs for the church, including 'Sing unto the Lord' and 'True Praises'.

Noel Robinson, who had been musical director for the Church of God of Prophecy, started to record his own albums, the first being *O Taste and See* released in 1993, followed by *Worthy in this Place*, *Garment of Praise*, *Devoted*, and the Integrity Music recording *Outrageous Love*. Noel has also overseen the worship at the Global

Day of Prayer stadium events, Maurice Cerullo events and Kingdom Renewal conferences.

LCGC celebrated their twenty-first anniversary in 2003 with an album and DVD recording live at Abbey Road Studios, with guests including Martin Smith, Matt Redman, Paul Carrack, Sam Moore and Carleen Anderson. This was a landmark evening, bringing together worship leaders and mainstream artists with this formidable choir.

Andraé Crouch regularly visited the UK, fathering the British Black gospel movement, before Israel Houghton arrived and introduced a new generational sound. In recent years, Israel and New Breed have brought a much loved multicultural flavour to the family music festival BigChurchDayOut.

Church leader Philip Mohabir, in his book *Building Bridges*, offered a prophetic challenge: 'Like the mustard seed in the parable, the black churches have grown into a significant force of Evangelical Christians, with a spontaneity, vibrancy and dynamism that the white constituency needs. Imagine what power for good we could be in the hand of God, if both communities could combine their resources and provide a prophetic witness to a nation that is in desperate need.'[5]

APOSTLES

Looking back over these years and the significant ways that God worked through people, it's clear that all of them benefitted from having a strong mentor, spiritual father and guide as they were starting out. For Dave Bilbrough, it was John Noble and Maurice Smith who fulfilled that role. Noel Richards and Ishmael had

Gerald Coates while Dave Fellingham was connected to Terry Virgo and Henry Tyler. For Chris Bowater it was Stuart Bell, while for Graham Kendrick it was Roger Forster and Clive Calver, and Bryn Haworth had the Vineyard movement.

International House of Prayer founder Mike Bickle is clear that these relationships are highly significant.

> The role of the apostle and the worship leader is very powerful. I don't claim to understand it fully, but I have a few ideas. I believe the apostolic ministries of people like Terry Virgo and Roger Forster are used to do more than just point to truths. They do so much more than that, introducing God's emphasis in a generation. Apostolic and prophetic preaching is grabbing the emphasis of God for a generation and bringing it to the forefront. They do that, and the songwriters write out of that overflow, creating an entire spiritual culture around those truths.

When asked how it feels as a teacher to have your words in the songs, Terry Virgo replied:

> That is a huge encouragement and I would say that is one of the things Dave Fellingham did from an early stage. Often after I'd preached something he'd come back with a song about it. Sometimes I asked him for a song. I remember when I was preaching on David at the Downs Bible Week, one

of the messages was on David's sin and I preached
on Psalm 51 and David's repentance. I said to
Dave 'I'd love a song about cleansing and forgive-
ness after sin'. He wrote me a most beautiful song
for that occasion. I feel he's hugely gifted at getting
hold of truth and putting it to music. It's been a
thrill to me. More recently some of the guys like
Nathan Fellingham have come up with songs on
the back of sermons we've preached.

One of the many unique things about the UK worship movement has been the closeness of the apostolic leader and the worship
leader. And it has carried on beyond the 1970s, with Mike Pilavachi
taking on the apostolic role to Matt Redman, Martyn Layzell and
Tim Hughes, with all of them writing songs that reflected his heart
and message.

Another unique characteristic is the unity and lack of competition between the worship leaders. They are a community without
being in competition with one another. The worship leaders are
not rivals, but friends.

A significant gathering of key worship leaders was organised by
Phil Rogers in 1985. Appropriately, this was held at Olney House,
home of the hymn writer John Newton. In attendance were Ian
Traynar, Chris Bowater, Dave Fellingham, Graham Kendrick, and
Dave Bilbrough. The group would grow, but this was the start
of many gatherings from which came friendships which were the
basis for the teaching teams for national worship conferences.

Chapter 5

THE 1980S—THE CROWDS GATHER

'I'd never seen anything like it in my life.' Helmut Kaufmann's memories of a visit he made to a British holiday camp remain perfectly clear decades on from the event. But this was no regular holiday that Helmut had stumbled upon. This was a Bible Week; a key part of the modern worship story.

Christians in the UK had been gathering to take part in Bible weeks for years. One of the most famous—the Keswick convention, held in the Lake District—traces its roots all the way back to 1875 and the revival that had spread throughout the nation at the time. But as the 1970s gave way to the 80s, things had changed a little. The basic formula remained the same, with different churches gathering together for a week of solid teaching from respected leaders, but as the times of sung worship became increasingly significant, so too did the opportunity for people to experience the charismatic side of things.

One of the first to make the transition to this new model was Capel Bible Week. According to Gerald Coates, 'it was a type of informal Keswick. It became more and more charismatic as Keswick became less and less charismatic.' He continues:

> There were no worship leaders back then. Even though we had people that sometimes would lead worship in their local church with a group of musicians, Barney Coombs and I used to lead. I'm not sure whether we didn't trust the others to lead a crowd of 2,000 people, whether they were just inexperienced or whether we were still besotted with the one-man ministry. It was a long time ago. Barney and I were church leader/ pastor type figures and so we led the worship together, without any instruments at all.

The event made a lasting impact on Dave Fellingham. 'That's where I first heard Dave Bilbrough's "Abba Father" and was incredibly impacted by the song. Hearing 1,000 people singing it was a profound experience for me.'

Under the direction of Arthur Wallis, Capel introduced freer styles of worship and praise. Bryn Jones then started a northern equivalent, initially called The Lakes and later the Dales Bible Week. As the new venture thrived, so Capel went into decline. Eventually, when Capel closed down in the late 1970s, Bryn Jones joined with Terry Virgo to start a new Bible week in the south of England, calling it Downs Bible Week. By the time it ended in the late 1980s it had regular crowds of 8,500 people.

Dave Fellingham was influenced strongly by Bradford and Basingstoke Community Churches: 'Both of these churches had a strong emphasis on worship, with worship being led by men in significant church leadership. Barney led worship as did his co-elder Vic Gledhill. It was Vic who was the main worship leader on a seminal worship album, *Praise Him Royal Priesthood*, put out by the Basingstoke church. It was this album that changed my whole understanding of worship.'[1]

The Dales Bible Week had been started by the Bradford church. The worship was mainly led by church leaders Keri Jones and Mike Stevens. The model then was that church leaders led worship, though by now they were supported by a band, rather than leading *a capella* or with a simple piano or organ. Dave Hadden led the band and was beginning to write songs. The Downs Bible Week grew out of this event, and was initially very influenced by Bryn Jones and his team, although Terry Virgo was clearly the leader.

There were other Bible weeks too, like Filey Bible Week, which had made such an impression on Helmut Kaufmann. He was there working with ICC, recording the seminars and providing the PA. From behind his tape deck he had ample time to notice the way the event worked. 'Lyndsay Clegg was the man there, and it was a tremendous event. Lyndsay had this vision of creating a Christian holiday, and the wonderful thing was that you had Pentecostals and Baptists all together. He had this knack of keeping them all together.'

After the death of Lyndsay Clegg in 1975, Filey returned to a more traditional approach, making way in 1979 for a new conference to emerge and thrive in a way few could ever have predicted. Launched in another holiday camp in Prestatyn, North Wales,

Spring Harvest drew 2,700 people in its first year. By 1990 this number had grown to around 80,000 in England and Scotland making it probably the largest residential event of its kind in the world, drawing people from every church background imaginable.[2] God was bringing His church together.

At the helm of the event were Clive Calver and Pete Meadows. 'Pete and I were trying to start an alternative to Keswick,' Clive explains, 'Not because we had anything against Keswick, but because we felt that our generation needed an expression of corporate spiritual life. Spring Harvest did not start off as a charismatic event; it started off as a teaching/training event. Its major thrust was young people and it embraced the worship songs of Graham Kendrick, who would write the theme songs, including classics "Servant King" and "Meekness and Majesty".'

Dave Pope also played a significant role in the worship at Spring Harvest, as Clive Calver explains:

> The great thing about Dave is that he has this beautiful flexibility of spirit. In the early days, people would say Graham Kendrick was charismatic and Dave wasn't, but very quickly Dave managed to build a bridge, probably more effectively at times than Graham did. He built this bridge to everybody and people felt very safe with Dave and could follow his lead. His lead took people further and further as he went further.
>
> Everyone said Spring Harvest was a charismatic event and we would all deny it, because

it really wasn't. You could look along the row at worshippers at Spring Harvest, and the first person may have their arms in the air, the next would have their hands in their pockets, the next at half mast, then maybe one dancing in the aisle while the next guy would be hanging onto their hymnbook for survival. There was this huge mix of people doing different things in different ways, and that was Spring Harvest at worship.

Pete Meadows saw the ways in which Clive, Graham and Dave complemented each other. 'Graham and Dave had a great contrast of styles. Graham was much more prophetic and Dave was slightly more traditional, but excellent. Clive had a passion for worship; he was and is a worshipper, always deeply influenced by Tozer. He dragged Graham with him into the arena of congregational worship and then Graham kept running!'

Writing in *Restoring the Kingdom*, Andrew Walker observed that 'Spring Harvest was dominated by the worship songs of Graham Kendrick, who, in my opinion, has had more influence on British Christianity than all the new church leaders put together.'[3]

Gerald Coates gained a unique perspective on the way in which Spring Harvest provided the house church leaders with a national platform:

> We were the bad guys; we were apostles who val-
> ued commitment to one another, rather than to
> Anglicanism or Baptism or Methodism. This was

all very challenging to the majority of Christians who were in mainline denominations, though many people were leaving established churches to join us in the house church movement.

What Clive and Pete did was to take who we were and to re-package it, so at Spring Harvest you had apostolic people on the platform but they didn't call them apostles. We had people prophesying on the platform but they didn't call them prophets. We had all the new church worship songs and eventually worship leaders leading worship—Dave Bilbrough, Noel Richards, Graham Kendrick and so on. A lot of the seminars were taken right out of new church theology, practice and different ways of doing things, but they re-packaged it, and I say that in a very positive way. They put it out there and sowed this seed to 80,000 people, which we could never have done.

I don't think we could have done what Clive and Pete did through Spring Harvest. It made people very impatient with local church and hungry for something more than the hymn/ prayer sandwich and the one-man ministry could provide.

Spring Harvest also modelled a change in the role of the worship leader. When Barney Coombs was in New Zealand, he had experienced a different model of worship leading. Instead of the church leader leading the worship David Garratt, leader of the worship team, would do this.

Up to this point in the UK, Barney Coombs and Gerald Coates would lead worship at Capel Bible Week, Keri Jones and Mike Stevens at Dales, and Dave Holden at Downs.

The Romford Fellowship were using the worship leader model with Dave Bilbrough, Ian Traynar and others, but it really became established at Spring Harvest, where Clive Calver had a strong friendship and trust with Graham Kendrick.

The strength of relationships between the worship leaders and church leaders, and the recognition of their gifting and sensitivity to how God was moving in the gathering, meant the worship leaders were given more and more responsibility and freedom.

For some prophets this has been frustrating. John Noble comments:

> At Spring Harvest, the assigning of the worship to the worship leader rather than the cooperation of the leadership team appears to have caused a lack of creativity.
>
> I think we need to see a return to ministries and worship leaders working closer together and giving way to each other. I think there is a kind of resignation that the worship leader can do it and that we won't interrupt them.
>
> The prophetic flow that used to take place where we gave way to each other was far greater

than I perceive it to be today. Often you have to
find a way in if you have something prophetic
to share.

This journey continues, but the model works well when
there are close relationships between church leaders and worship
leaders.

Meanwhile, God was powerfully at work in other Bible weeks.
The Downs Bible Week was thriving, with Dave Fellingham and
Phil Rogers developing worship within what eventually became
the Newfrontiers church movement. Phil was one of the first
to put on musicians' training days, bringing people together,
emphasising the value of teamwork and unity.

Dave Fellingham was able to see the way the worship reflected
what was being preached: 'There was a huge connection between
worship and the prophetic movement. We were singing what
we were seeing; songs about the church, about our peoplehood,
about the kingdom. It was a very significant time.'

At first, the singing was accompanied just by a piano, but as
Dave remembered,

> The second year things opened up a little with
> Terry's leadership of the event more visible. He
> introduced more worship leaders, who were guys
> leading churches. Musical skill was certainly not
> a consideration. The third year saw an intro-
> duction of a few more instruments and I ended
> up leading worship for most of the sessions.

That was when more orchestral musicians were added and under the direction of Phil Rogers the embryonic Downs orchestra began. The next year, 1982, there were so many people wanting to play that we had to filter who was going to be involved. This was the year when I orchestrated all the songs rather than just letting the accompaniments be improvised. The Downs orchestra was established this year and for the next three years was an integral part of Downs worship.

Around this time other Bible weeks started to spring up across the UK, including Grapevine, South and West Bible Week, Royal Week and Kingdom Faith Bible Week. Generally, a live album would be recorded at each of these Bible weeks.

According to Mike Bickle, another reason for the significance of Bible weeks like the Downs, which went on to become Stoneleigh, was the sheer size. 'It wasn't just that Terry Virgo preached on three things and two songwriters grabbed it. This was a movement of thousands of people. The leaders used their apostolic authority and their position in the Spirit to impart these truths in a way that multitudes could receive. I think that's the greatest thing about these events; the gathering anointing. It is only ever by that anointing that the songs spread out.'

Of all the things that people notice about the UK worship movement, one of the most distinctive elements is the strength of community. Those Bible weeks clearly laid good foundations, as David Ruis points out:

Psalm 133:1 reminds us that there is a blessing to be found in unity. God commands a blessing of such force that no man or alliance of darkness can stop it. It's commanded—it's like a wave that crashes everything in its resistance.

As a Canadian it was really refreshing to have more of a community kind of feel of things, people in tents and hanging out together, eating together and laughing. That's tremendous. To me it as much feeds the integrity of the worship experience as anything else. I don't know what plays into it [in the UK], but there's a deep passion to find community, and I think there is at least a pursuit of that which is touching the blessing on the worship. I think this is a significant piece— the pursuit of community and relationship and finding ways to co-operate together.

So many worship experiences in the UK have revolved around community—Spring Harvest, all of these things. And I think that's scriptural, the blessing of God rests there. There's a depth. Maybe, too, that allows for a corporate body to declare together, it's very intimate, very real. The North American thing has been a lot more individual, and I think the understanding of the corporateness of worship is still a whole area to be looked at and cultivated. But the UK's way ahead on that.

In the mid-80s there was also a real synergy between the UK and South Africa, who were both exploring similar strands of truth. Malcolm Du Plessis, a worship leader from Cape Town, visited the UK and was impacted by the boldness and audacity for the priesthood of all believers. 'I loved the fact that there were songs of content. I found a joy in singing these songs that had much more substance and it was inspiring to me.'

Previously, in 1983, Malcolm had been inspired to write songs himself. He remembers:

> I thought that since we only get songs from other places, perhaps we should write our own. Then I met these guys from England [who were visiting South Africa], and their commitment to writing songs was an inspiration and provocation to me. It was catalytic in terms of inspiring me to think, 'Why don't we do the same? Let's get all our people and write our own songs.'
>
> Terry Virgo came to South Africa to speak at a city-wide event and we sang a song I'd written called 'We Declare Your Majesty'. Terry was very impacted by it and asked for a recording of it—he took it back to his church and it became the theme song for Downs Bible Week in 1985.

Mike Bickle enjoyed seeing the Bible weeks develop and appreciated Stoneleigh greatly.

The worship was the thing that hit you. I remember the spontaneous singing in the congregation, the singing in the Spirit, the intimacy and majesty songs and the songs of the Lord on the platform.

These Bible weeks often have the gathering anointing. The songs get sent out to the whole world along the highways and byways. Granted, there are the big Wembley Stadium deals, but if there weren't the Bible weeks, those worship leaders would never have been known. The apostolic ministries create the culture and they emphasise the present truths on God's heart and create a culture where thousands embody them. So it's a living reality.

One feature of the Bible weeks was the extended times of singing spontaneously in the Spirit. These moments were known as the 'Song of the Lord'.

As Mike Bickle remembers:

Terry Virgo was the one—with Arthur Wallis— that convinced me that [speaking in] tongues was of God. And then Terry taught me about the song of the Lord, I was just in my early twenties and I was just so excited about it, I ran with it and devoted my life to it—from Terry Virgo. Twenty years later we started International House of Prayer (IHOP).

I spent a month with Terry Virgo, Arthur Wallis and Tony Morton, under Bryn Jones' leadership, in 1978. I became dear friends with Terry—I love Terry. The next year they all came and spoke at our church. In 1978 the choruses were just coming out, mostly celebration, not much intimacy, not much majesty, but biblical. It was always biblical. In America in the late 70s the choruses were not anti-biblical or anti-truth, but they were not necessarily biblical language. But the UK took it beyond celebration. Wimber's ministry was, I think, incalculable in terms of its impact with intimacy. But then they added majesty with intimacy and took it to another level.

Here's the interesting thing. Terry Virgo and Arthur Wallis teach Mike Bickle in 1978 that tongues is of God. They taught me from 1 Corinthians 14, line by line. They took me through it for several hours and taught me the song of the Lord. Then they came and taught in my church in 1980, in which there were David Ruis and Kevin Prosch. They weren't even full-time worship leaders in our church when they first came. They were musicians, just hanging around and then they started leading worship in the prayer meetings with twenty to thirty people for a year first, before leading on Sunday mornings for another year or two and before they were asked to lead at conferences. I gave them Terry Virgo's stuff!

I'm not saying that David Ruis and Kevin Prosch got all of their insight from being with us at Kansas City. They had obviously many things burning in them long before that, but that's where they were launched into international platforms, out of Kansas City, and it was all formed around Terry Virgo's teaching. Terry came over a number of times to teach for us, so Terry's teaching influenced Kevin Prosch, and Kevin Prosch sang over Matt Redman!

MARCH FOR JESUS

The power of unity didn't just reside in the numerous holiday camps and county showgrounds up and down the country that served as venues for the many Bible weeks. At the same time that the crowds were flocking to these events, Graham Kendrick was dreaming up something wholly different.

> This first wave of praise and worship was happening all over the place, and many churches were adopting the new style of worship and so on. I felt there was a serious danger that we were neglecting the church's mission; that we were now having a great time in church and that was where it was ending. Surely true worship must

relate to the mission of the church and touching
the world? What a tragedy if we were just having
a great time behind our four walls, and the world
didn't even know we were there, unless we had
the windows open occasionally.

Ichthus, Graham's home church, was doing a lot of street
outreach, and soon after he joined Graham had taken part in a
mission in Peckham, south east London.

I just joined a team going knocking on doors on
these housing estates and singing on the streets
and stuff, most of which I struggled with; I just
find those things hard to do. This whole thing
began to grow and I was aware that organisations
like Youth With A Mission were experimenting
with worship on the streets and prayer walks.
With these thoughts in mind, I joined a couple
of hundred other people one Saturday night on a
prayer walk around Soho, which was at that time
the red light district of London.

I don't think any of us had ever done this
before, so we didn't have any particular methodology. We tried to do what we did indoors,
outdoors. It was in the course of that evening that
it was really confirmed to me, that although this
was outside my comfort zone, and my tempera-
ment meant I didn't like it at all, in my spirit I felt

sure that it was something we should be doing. I instinctively knew it was an effective means of prayer and preparing the way for establishing ministry in an area, as well as a witness.

I also observed that we needed a methodology for it, and that a lot of the songs that we used on that evening, which were perfectly valid in church, didn't really work too well. You'd end up choosing the liveliest praise song you could think of and then feel that it must be nonsense to the people around—a kind of coded language.

And then it was a question of finding a methodology with instruments, because how do you actually play together? On the streets the sound disappears up into the air, and what instruments are best suited?

I went home, having decided I was going to try and write a series of songs. These became the embryo of what was to become March For Jesus.

I set out to make and record a whole sequence of music, scripture verses and shouts that would be easy to use and simple to learn. I borrowed a few ideas from what I had seen at several street events, trying to understand the dynamics of a crowd of people spread down the street. I wanted to create something that could, without endless practices and rehearsals, unite a whole crowd in prayer and proclamation.

This first *Make Way* album was released at Easter 1986. We accompanied it with a small booklet giving some practical instructions on how to take praise onto the streets. From our limited experience, we tackled some of the difficulties of welding together a crowd of people strung out along the street, the technicalities of making the music work and the basic organisational necessities.

When the whole vision was taken up with tremendous enthusiasm, I was genuinely surprised. Churches were writing to say they were learning all the songs, using the contents of the instruction book and actually taking it onto the streets around the country. What delighted me even more were the reports of churches from different denominations and traditions joining together to do this thing. Even more conservative ones were joining in. There seemed to be a mood swing in the churches, a sense that the time was right.

Gerald Coates remembers: 'Graham and Roger Forster [his leader at Ichthus] came to Lynn Green, who headed up YWAM, and myself from Pioneer, saying that they wanted to put on a march in the spring of 1987.'

That City March was held in pouring rain. On the morning of the event Gerald Coates was concerned about how successful it would be.

I can remember saying to Noel 'Who on earth is going to come today?' We'd hoped that 2,000 would come and as the day approached we had heard that there would be nearer to 5,000. When we arrived there were probably 1,500 to 2,000 people in the pouring rain. At the start time I had a note passed to me saying that the police were now going to open the doors. We were in the open air and I thought 'What doors? What are they talking about?' In front of me was a railway viaduct and all the arches had had these huge doors put on them and they'd been made into little workshops. What I didn't know was that to keep the crowd dry the police had put people into the workshops. When they opened all the doors 15,000 people poured out.

The event was a success, but Gerald was clear on one thing: that was the first and last City March. There wasn't going to be another one.

But of course, the following year it happened again. Only this time, between 45,000 and 55,000 turned out to what was now called March For Jesus. It was unforgettable to see thousands of marchers streaming over London's Westminster and Hungerford Bridges, to gather on the Embankment for a March For Jesus to the heart of the nation in 1988. Graham says,

This was a historic moment in seeing the UK church mobilised to worship and pray on the

streets, and reminded us of the verses in
Psalm 68:24–26:

'Your procession, God, has come into view,
    the procession of my God and King into the
        sanctuary.
In front are the singers, after them the
        musicians;
    with them are the young women playing the
        tambourines.
Praise God in the great congregation.'

After that, Gerald knew that the growth was unstoppable.

I think part of the reason was because Roger,
Lynn, Graham and I made a decision very early
on that we would not profit financially or in
terms of reputation from March For Jesus. We
were in the London programme and our faces
were photographed, but there was no big 'Now
ladies and gentleman: Gerald Coates or Roger
Forster'. It wasn't like that. In the 120 nations
that hosted a march, ninety-nine per cent of the
people on the streets had no clue who we were or
whether we were even involved.

In their book about March For Jesus, Graham Kendrick,
Gerald Coates, Roger Forster and Lynn Green write the following:

The rise of March For Jesus was phenomenal. In 1990 it spread to the USA and South Africa, and even though the Berlin Wall was still standing and half the continent was governed by communist regimes, the team started to dream of a European march. On 23 May 1992 more than 250,000 Europeans took to the streets in such places as Moscow, Gdansk, Warsaw, Prague, Budapest, Bucharest and Tirana, as well as many Western European capitals.

Reconciliation and unity were key themes in the forty-seven European marches. Christians in the Cypriot capital of Nicosia marched to the green line dividing Greek and Turkish Cyprus and prayed for reconciliation. In the Polish city of Gdansk, Protestants and Roman Catholics joined in equal numbers to march together through the city—the first ever sign of unity between the two groups.

About 6,000 marchers took to the streets of Prague on the day—both Czechs and Slovaks— and their script included prayers for their General Election. Organisers said 'We do not remember a joint activity of such a broad spectrum of churches. We are looking forward to the march next year.'

In Berlin 60,000 Christians marched for Jesus along Unter den Linden and through the

Brandenberg gate; the same route that Hitler had used to parade the might and power of the Third Reich. Most of the Christian denominations were represented in joyful and colourful celebration, which was an impressive sign of the changes taking place in Germany. In Vienna, Protestant and Catholic leaders prayed together about divisions in the church. The Mayor of Vienna commented: 'I believe in the power of faith. It's exactly the power that is missing in today's world.'

Turkish Christians were not allowed to march, so they held a 'Sail for Jesus'! In Istanbul about 100 adults plus children hired a boat and sailed up the Bosporus which divides Europe from Asia. They stopped on the Asian side near some mosques to pray, then sailed back to the European side for a time of worship.

Christians in Tirana, Albania, were particularly glad to be able to take part in an international event. The Tirana march started in the city's main park on the plinth where the statue of Stalin once stood. By the time the 300 marchers reached Tirana's main square numbers had grown to between 2,000 and 3,000.

Christians in Moscow also took part and were glad to be involved in an initiative which allowed them to be Russians rather than to receive Western teaching. The Moscow marchers—500 in all—left the rallying point two miles from the Kremlin led by dancers in Russian costumes. Dougie Brown, a worship leader from the UK who was in the city for the event, said that seeing 'hundreds of Spirit-filled Russian Christians freely glorifying God on the street was almost too much. I was seeing with my eyes what I had seen in my heart for twenty-four years. I couldn't believe I was seeing it.'

Even in war-torn Yugoslavia fifty people gathered to pray in Belgrade and were planning to bring Evangelicals, Catholics and Orthodox church members together for a march at a later date.[4]

Another major highpoint was the Global March For Jesus in 1994, which saw a march happen in every time zone of the world, involving ten million Christians from over 170 nations.

Graham started the day being part of the march in Christchurch, New Zealand before crossing over the International Date Line to Western Samoa for the final march of the day.

It was a memorable day which saw Psalm 113:3 fulfilled: 'From the rising of the sun to the place where it sets, the name of the LORD is to be praised.'

Between the first march in 1987 and the last in 2000, an estimated sixty million people in 180 nations took to the streets to pray, praise and demonstrate their faith.[5] The Brazilian church adopted the march as their carnival, and this resulted in 1.2 million Christians taking to the streets to celebrate. Even now, in Sao Paulo, one of the largest cities in the world, March For Jesus is a public holiday.

A key part of March For Jesus was the worship. Though it sounded as though it had been written purposefully for the march, 'Rejoice! Rejoice!' which was originally on the *Let God Arise* album, had been written by Graham two or three years before it all started.

> At the time of writing it I didn't have a specific vision of the street processions that became March For Jesus. It was simply an exhortation and metaphor to get out there—for the church to rise up and fulfil its destiny.
>
> At the time there was a need for the church to wake up, be more active and believe that God can actually do things that will affect our neighbourhoods, our towns and the nations. There was a need to be more confident and to be a little stronger in the face of evil, unbelief and the problems that face us.

With so many people taking part in such a dramatically different and Spirit-led event, it is unsurprising that many believe March For Jesus played a deeply significant role in the story of evangelical Christianity.

Andrew Walker describes the first March For Jesus:

> The first national march, which was on 16 September 1989, was supported by the Evangelical Alliance and saw nearly a quarter of a million people take to the streets. A great deal of hard work

and enterprise went into the event but much of the
success was due to Graham Kendrick's imaginative
processional liturgy—Make Way.

The structure was ideal for street celebration
using a fairly traditional antiphonal structure in
which the leader called out such phrases as 'Make
way, make way' and 'Prepare the way of the Lord'
while the crowds responded accordingly.[6]

The March For Jesus albums took the form of side one being
songs of worship, preparation and intercession, and the second
side being a soundtrack and songs for the streets.

The first album was called *Carnival of Praise*, and was followed
by *Make Way for the King of Kings*, *Make Way for Christmas*, *Make
Way for the Cross* and *King of the Nations*. *Make Way for the King of
Kings* included the song 'Shine, Jesus, Shine', which would become
a worship and prayer anthem resonating with the church in many
nations.

David Ruis is convinced that March For Jesus had a lasting
impact. 'I'm definitely sure there were seeds planted through
Graham and through the march. It broadened the understanding
of the part worship plays in advancing the kingdom of God. It's
not just what happens in a room or when a few gather, it's part of
how the kingdom of God moves across the earth. So the seeds of
that begin to stir and I think in a lot of ways it's blown into full
flame by just living in intercession.' March For Jesus was the first
UK movement to go way beyond these shores and to have global
impact and bless the nations of the world.

Louie and Shelley Giglio (leaders of the student movement Passion) received a revelation of worship at the Baptist Youth Conference in Glasgow in 1988. 'During this conference, songs like 'Shine, Jesus, Shine', and the public proclamation of worship happening in March For Jesus made a huge impact on us, propelling us forward in declarative, prophetic worship for cities and nations.'

For Mike Bickle the link between March For Jesus and the successful evangelistic Alpha Course is clear: 'That Britain prays and then Alpha breaks and millions get saved ... I think those two are connected. Think about that five-year period; there were masses of people united on the streets, prayer walking and then, boom! The greatest grassroots evangelism thing we've ever seen, Alpha. I think it's linked. Absolutely linked. I couldn't prove it, but I would be shocked in heaven if it wasn't linked.'

Chapter 6

JOHN WIMBER AND VINEYARD MUSIC

It started as soon as he landed at Heathrow. John Wimber, the former musician who had given everything up in pursuit of an adventure with God, found himself out cold on the London tarmac, knocked down by the power of the Holy Spirit as soon as he had stepped off the plane. 'God, why have you done this?' he asked.

'Because I am giving you this land.'[1]

In the years that followed, God made good on His promise. John Wimber became as influential a figure on the UK worship scene as any featured in this book. And it was no understatement for Terry Virgo to say following John's death in 1997, 'next to Billy Graham, the man who influenced the British church the most was John Wimber.'[2]

John had been a talented and successful musician from early on in life. In 1962 he was involved in the founding of the Righteous Brothers, a duo who eventually supported The Beatles. John played saxophone in their backing band, yet shortly after his conversion, he knew that the Lord was telling him to lay down all that he had built for himself as a successful musician. 'Give me everything,' God said. 'Liquidate all your assets and I'll give you the pearl: the pearl is Jesus.'[3]

John went on to establish the Vineyard church in Anaheim, California. Phil Lawson-Johnson, a worship leader at Holy Trinity Brompton between 1975 and 1990, paid an early visit there, where he met fellow worship leader Carl Tuttle.

> I always remember him telling the story of when they started the Vineyard, which was just a home-group really, [consisting of] John and a few other burnt-out leaders. Carl was there and was the only one who could play anything, so he was appointed as the worship leader. He said himself that he wasn't a very good guitarist, and he could only play a few chords and had written some really simple love songs to the Lord. When the church began to grow and they moved into new premises people came in and Carl saw a number of much better musicians coming into the church. He went to John Wimber and said he thought it was time he asked one of them to play because they were so much better than he was. I think John said no and that Carl was the guy that the Lord had anointed for this, and that they've got to learn to become worshippers first. It's quite an important principle when you're appointing people.

Like so many others, Phil was impacted by how different worship was at the Vineyard.

> It was really the friendship and closeness of the songs that drew us into meeting with the Lord. I already knew the thing about whether we're singing about God or to Him because David Watson was always strong about singing 'a song unto the Lord', instead of just about Him. We were aware of that, but at the Vineyard nearly all the songs were addressed to God or Jesus.
>
> We'd sung the sort of triumph, the glory and the praise and all the rest of it but they added another dimension, which was the intimacy side.

It was a deliberate move on John's part. He constantly encouraged the church to pursue intimacy in worship, something he described as the highest and most fulfilling calling that men and women may know. He placed worship firmly at the top of the new church's agenda, declaring that, 'Our first priority is to give God's love back to Him'. As a result, the Vineyard model of worship introduced a new expectancy to meet with God intimately through song.

Word about what was happening in the Vineyard church spread, eventually reaching the ears of Eddie Gibbs, a British academic teaching about church growth at the Fuller Seminary in Pasadena. Before he left the UK, Eddie had been asked by his home vicar, David Pytches, to let him know if he encountered anyone who he felt could move the church, St Andrew's Chorleywood, on. So when David Pytches and David Watson travelled to Fuller Seminary to teach on the Doctor of Ministry course, Eddie Gibbs made sure that both Davids met up with John Wimber. A true friendship formed, and John was soon invited to visit the UK.

According to Graham Cray, John's relationship with the Church of England was special and built on key relationships that he formed here. 'He respected the leadership that he found in the Renewal in the Church of England. He just wanted to pour what God had given Vineyard into that. He was also impacted by the concept of a parish church being in walking distance of every resident in Britain.'

In 1981, on his first ministry visit to the UK, John and team came to David Watson's church—St Michael Le Belfrey, York— and St Andrew's Chorleywood, home to a young Matt Redman:

> I was only seven at the time, but I was taken along to the meeting at church. Those songs just ushered in a fresh intimacy which I'd never experienced in church worship and music. I was really drawn to the idea that you cannot only sing to God and He hears our songs and you can bless the heart of God through songs, but there's actually another dimension where you can engage with God through songs. You can meet Him and draw near to Him through music and He draws near to you.[4]

St Andrew's became known as a church that was comfortable with taking risks for God, as Matt discovered: 'I've been really privileged to be in an environment where I've been encouraged. I was encouraged as a young person to really go for it. Mike Pilavachi was my youth pastor and David Pytches was my vicar, and they encouraged me to step out and go for it. They affirmed me, and just being in an environment where I could be introduced to the Vineyard stuff was really significant.'

Mike Pilavachi saw that Wimber's visit had come at just the right moment. 'As far as the renewal in the historic churches was concerned, Wimber and the teaching he brought in those early days was like a new lease of life. For those of us in the Anglican church, he gave us a model that combined Pentecostal power with evangelical theology and used a style that was low key, humorous, [and] avoided hype and manipulation. We had been waiting to see the power of God expressed in a model like that, and when we saw it we loved it.'

David Pytches and David Watson were not the only ones to visit from the UK and come back inspired. Phil Lawson-Johnson recalls the impact that a visit to California had on his vicar at HTB, Sandy Millar.

> At HTB we had started an evening service and we'd gone quite far down the line with worship. But in California at a Vineyard conference, Sandy caught the vision for worship. He returned saying, 'Worship is going to be our number one priority. We're going to worship in our small groups, in our pastorate groups, whenever we get together we are going to worship.' In some

cases worship had been regarded as the warm up
for the important thing, which was the sermon.
When the congregation saw that Sandy was fully
engaged and worshiping away, it gave a message
to everyone that this was important. This was key
in transforming the worship culture of HTB.

John was used by God to usher in a fresh approach to worship. He offered the church a biblical and practical framework for
approaching the Lord through song. At the heart of what John and
the Vineyard church were exploring in worship was the sense that
they should be rooted in a relationship with Jesus. Years later, at a
Vineyard worship leaders gathering, I saw John interrupt a discussion about the global impact of Vineyard songs. He then pointed
out that there were a couple of aspects of God's character that weren't
being included in the songs, and pointed to a few piles of books on
those subjects. He encouraged his worship leaders to go and choose
the books, read them, and write songs on those themes.

Not everyone in the UK appreciated Vineyard's style of worship straight away. Dave Fellingham wasn't sold at first.

When I first heard Vineyard worship I didn't
really like it musically and I found it a bit too
touchy-feely. But that was hearing the music
before I'd met John Wimber. Having met him
and seen him in that worship dynamic, I think
they brought something that was very significant, and now I've grown to really love Vineyard

music. I think it does have its limitations, but I
think they have made contributions to the worship scene that are incredibly significant. John
Wimber was a great worshipper, and I used to
love to sit down on a one-to-one with him and
talk about worship. He had such a heart for
God and musicians and worship leaders. It was
just a great privilege to know him and to work
with him.

I think one of the things that the Vineyard
did was to bring a standard of excellence in their
bands and in their music, alongside the content
and the songs. [They were] such good players
and vocalists, and well produced recordings.

These songs and arrangements were easily replicated and
within reach of the local church musician.

Stuart Townend felt similarly, and remembers being 'completely amazed and impacted by early Vineyard recordings, albums
like *Just Like You Promised* and *You Are Here*.'

Three years after his first visit, John and his team returned to
the UK to host the Third Wave conference in Westminster Central
Hall. This proved to be monumental in bringing mainstream char-
ismatics and house church leaders together. In Terry Virgo's mind,
'John Wimber renewed the renewal.'

Mike Pilavachi was there too. 'Carl Tuttle led the worship on
a beat up old guitar and I loved Wimber's teaching and ministry,
but the thing that completely unhinged me was the worship. It was

just simple, passionate love songs to Jesus. I broke. It was so fresh and real. That became our new template for worship.'

Andrew Walker later wrote that 'John Wimber became a major force in British Christianity, especially among Anglicans. I do not think it's an exaggeration to say that Wimber and the style and methodology of the Vineyard fellowships has been the greatest influence in mainstream renewal since the ministry of the late canon David Watson and the hey-day of the Fountain Trust.'[5]

In time there were many more visits from John to the UK, and as his home worship team grew and new churches were planted, so other names emerged within the Vineyard movement. Carl Tuttle, Eddie Espinosa, Andy Park, Cindy Reithmeier and others were joined in time by the likes of Kevin Prosch, Brian Doerksen and David Ruis. With a recording studio at their church in Anaheim, California, they recorded the *Touching the Father's Heart* albums, releasing a new one every few months.

Bit by bit, the Vineyard's reputation as a new worship movement grew. Brian Doerksen saw the impact first-hand, frequently traveling to the UK as part of the Vineyard worship team.

> It was amazing when I first got here and I saw how people would flock to hear John speak. I watched how the songs were beginning to influence the church. When I started coming I was just involved in my local church and had no idea what I was getting myself into. All of a sudden, here you are amongst thousands of people in England, leading worship and you're

pinching yourself and wondering how you got
here. By the mercy and favour of God, I guess.

God communicated to John clearly that he
had opened the door for favour in England. And
I think there were a number of Anglican leaders
who with great courage welcomed John and the
ministry of the Holy Spirit, because they could
trust John and trusted his theology. They realised that he was not throwing out the Word.

Mike Bickle saw it too. 'The church in the UK said yes to the
emphasis that John put on intimacy in worship. The church here
took it, but then added a sense of God's majesty to it. Intimacy
by itself is wonderful, majesty by itself is wonderful, but the two
together is unique. It's a synergism and the UK put that together.
It was the first place in the world to do that.'

That synergy meant that the American visitors were as impacted
by their travels as their UK hosts. Terry Virgo remembers sitting
next to John at a worship conference in Brighton: 'We were singing
one of Noel and Tricia Richards' songs. John was just crying and
his whole body was shaking and tears were falling down his face.
He said, "That song was written in heaven."' Eventually Noel and
Tricia's song 'All Heaven Declares' was included on a *Touching the
Father's Heart* album in 1991, even though it meant John breaking
the protocol of only having Vineyard copyrights on their albums.

David Ruis, who didn't start out within the Vineyard, observed
the impact the movement had on the UK. 'The thing that did
surprise me was the Anglican receptivity to the Vineyard. To see a

historic mainline segment of the church casting off all their trappings and embracing the essence of what was happening with this worship model for ministry was tremendous.'

As much as these early visits impacted and encouraged established worship leaders like Noel, Graham and Dave Fellingham, the greatest impact was on those too young to really lead at the time. These were ones whom Mike Bickle describes as 'the new wave of young people that had the intimacy and majesty thing in their music, but who also had the new sound on top of that. Soul Survivor is phenomenal. Our Kansas City group—we drink from the England well big time.'

Graham Cray felt that without the influence of John Wimber and Fisherfolk that impacted York and David Watson, 'Soul Survivor wouldn't be here, it's the fruit of all these things flowing together'— an opinion that Mike Pilavachi shared:

> We've learnt not to try and keep to that style, but the values are something which remained with many of us. That's what brought the Anglican and denominational renewal movements with the new church stuff together. I think Wimber caused us to become friends.
>
> We now work very closely with all the church movements. We recognise each other because we have what he and the Vineyard brought us, as part of our common heritage.
>
> With worship it was massive. Wimber introduced Kevin Prosch to us and others. We realised

that we needed to run with it. There was Martin
Smith writing some great worship songs; Matt
Redman and others started writing worship songs.
That was huge for us because it became authentic.

Graham Cray agrees: 'The worship from Soul Survivor and
Delirious? seems to have been yet another gift from God. A gift way
beyond the culture of this country.'

Chapter 7

———

SONGS OF FELLOWSHIP
AND OTHER RESOURCES

As much as the Holy Spirit was shaking up church services, there were also significant changes taking place throughout the wider church world. The early 80s were marked by innovative ideas which led to a growth in new resources, record labels and publishing companies, as well as conferences, songbooks and teaching. One of these developments by forward-thinking churches was the use of overhead projectors to project the song words onto screens. This was revolutionary and made it possible for new songs to spread from church to church rather than waiting years for the next edition of a songbook. By 1983 this had become widely accepted, and by 1985 was an alternative to standard songbooks.

The result was a sharp improvement in the ways in which worship leaders and songwriters were equipped and inspired.

One of the key players within all of this was Geoff Shearn who, almost two decades earlier, had been a founder member of MGO (Musical Gospel Outreach). Having now moved on from his role at Kingsway, Geoff had become Graham Kendrick's manager and had also formed the Christian Music Association (CMA) and Just Music, both of which would go on to become significant influences in the world of worship.

As the appetite for Christian music in the mainstream started to dry up, MGO found itself getting behind a small recording project from a church in Cobham attended by Nigel Coltman, Geoff's right hand man at MGO.

It was a simple affair, featuring contemporary worship songs that were popular throughout UK churches. It was recorded over a couple of weekends, but the album—*A New Song*—sold over 40,000 units over the next ten years. A second album, *City of God*, followed, and at some point the discussion turned to releasing an accompanying songbook.

By this time MGO had moved to Eastbourne and started to forge a close partnership with Kingsway, a Christian book publisher. Wandering around their warehouses one day, Nigel Coltman spotted something that made him stop.

> It was a box of pink-covered songbooks called *Songs of Fellowship*. I thought it was a great title, and wondered if it was available. It turned out that the songbook had originally been put out by Fountain Trust but was no longer being published. After talking to Geoff I contacted Fountain Trust and said we'd like to use it as a title, and asked if they would mind. It was round about the time they were thinking of winding up anyway and they said it wasn't a problem. So our very first

songbook, which had fifty-three songs, was called
Songs of Fellowship.

One thing Geoff and the team liked about the title was that 'it
was felt to be a little bit of a link with the house fellowships, but also
it was a non-threatening phrase.'

The book was published by Kingsway Books, and CWR
(Crusade for World Revival) placed an order for half of the initial
print run. Volume 1 quickly became a bestseller. Geoff Shearn says:

> It was very encouraging to Kingsway and we
> agreed then to go on and produce a more substan-
> tial volume. The hunt for worship songs grew in
> earnest and we started to look all over the place to
> find the best worship songs.
>
> Gradually we got to know different writers
> around the country—church leaders Gerald
> Coates, John Noble, Peter Fenwick and others
> were incredibly supportive and were introducing
> us left, right and centre to new songwriters and
> new songs. Our job seemed to be to gather these
> songs together to extend them out to the main-
> stream part of the church.

Dave Roberts was also involved in the project. '*Songs of
Fellowship* gathered momentum very quickly and by 1984 and
1985 there were a couple of hundred songs within the offering.'
Peter Fenwick says:

I would regard Geoff Shearn as a very important player in the development of worship and
the spread of worship through the churches.
Kingsway obviously became thoroughly known
as the worshipping company; the worship label.
We had a traditional form of worship, which
the likes of Kendrick fitted into very well, and
Bilbrough and Richards and others. Geoff [also]
had a great team supporting him including Nigel
Coltman and Pat Herridge.

A quarter of a century later *Songs of Fellowship* songbooks have
sold over 600,000 copies worldwide, and become a major instru-
ment in resourcing the church with new songs. But the project has
done far more than teach lyrics and chord progressions, which Dave
Roberts also credits to Geoff Shearn: 'Geoff developed the idea that
a lot of churches would appreciate a very broad ranged resource, so
he wrote down some things about what it should be, and one of
the phrases that was written down was "much more than a songbook." His team picked up on this phrase and ran with it, eventually
branching out into seminars, and recordings of every song.' The
songs included in the book quickly became the songs of the UK
worship movement.

Stuart Townend took on the editorial role on *Songs of
Fellowship* in the late 1980s, by which time it was already crossing
denominations. 'There was a sense of all being in this together.
Events like Spring Harvest were drawing people from all the
different streams and people were learning to be open to one

another. The songs were all going out and it didn't matter that this song came from somebody who was in a house church or an Anglican church; the songs were expressing a movement that was cross-denominational.'

WORSHIP CONFERENCES

It wasn't just *Songs of Fellowship* that was experiencing growth. This was a season of multiplication for worship conferences. Conferences put on by the Vineyard as well as other churches helped musicians and worship leaders to be trained, equipped and inspired.

Dave Roberts, initially brought on as A&R (Artists and Repertoire) Manager at Kingsway went on to play a key role in the development and organisation of worship seminars. He had already gained experience organising seminars for artists, influenced by Francis Schaeffer from L'Abri. Ian Traynar from the Romford Fellowship also played a key role and went on to work closely with the Christian Music Association organising conferences around Britain.

According to Dave, it all started when Ray Bodkin, a key member of the Kingsway staff, said,

> 'We've got 750 people on our *Songs of Fellowship*
> update list. Why don't we put on a worship con-
> ference?' We did and in 1984 we went to Pilgrim
> Hall, Eastbourne and it was totally booked out.
> It was an incredible weekend because Graham
> Kendrick shared on spiritual warfare and

Jehoshaphat, explaining that worshippers can go ahead of the army and see the battle won. We had these long extended times of worship where Graham did a lot of improvisation, and out of it came a song, 'We Are Marching', which was on the *Magnificent Warrior* album.

It was a very formative time for me, as well as a lot of the delegates I think. From that point on we never looked back; worship conferences were what we did. At one of them Graham introduced 'Here Is Love, Vast as the Ocean', reminding us that we needed the new but that we should also value the old.

There was one memorable conference at High Leigh where we really did experiment with everything; mime, art, drama. In many ways you would look back on it now and say it was commonplace or ordinary, but at the time it didn't feel like that at all. It felt like we were breaking out of the pews and the hymn-prayer sandwich and were exploring a more complete way of expressing ourselves to God.

In 1988, at Camber, we had about 1,600 people with a strong line up of speakers, Terry Virgo and Roger Forster amongst others. It was also quite marked because seventy of the delegates were Roman Catholics, and there were a wide variety of spectrums within the Roman

Catholic movement. Dave Fellingham said the significant thing for him was that there were so many overseas people there. What was going on in Britain was attracting interest from around the world.

By that time, we were beginning to mature in terms of our ability to gauge what would be helpful to the delegates. So it was very practical at one level, and it was one of the first times we did a PA stream: a lot of churches had moved from piano, guitar and organ, and were now facing a situation where they had multi-instrument groups and they were using public address systems, and it was a bit of a neglected area.

This was a season for multiplication of worship conferences, alongside the Vineyard events. Multitudes of musicians, worship leaders and teams were being trained, equipped and inspired.

In the midst of all this growth, a further key development was about to take place, involving Chris Bowater.

We had already been doing Together for Jesus tours, with people like Sue Rinaldi, Noel Richards, myself, Wes Sutton, Phil Lawson-Johnson and Dave Hadden: guys that would not often get together actually touring together.

It was very low key and there was never a major shop window for it, but I remember in Norwich we filled a huge centre with about 1,800 people, with churches coming together who had never been together before in the area.

By this time, John Pac had moved on from his role as A&R Manager at Pilgrim Records. He and his wife, Juliet, had moved to Eastbourne as he had taken up the role of head of Kingsway Music. It was an exciting time with thousands of worship leaders and musicians being trained up, and key worship leaders moving into the role of teachers. This model would develop into Worship Together conferences.

Once in Eastbourne, John and Juliet met up with Chris Bowater. 'I remember going down to see John Pac and Robert Lamont (former Head of Publishing for Word Music). The way I work is that I'm always looking at how to train and equip worship leaders, and I was convinced that there was a way forward of not only networking what God was doing, but communicating and building on it. So we talked about releasing new songs and starting a quarterly magazine.'

The idea took off, and *Worship Together* was born. Soon it gave birth to one-day conferences that were hosted around the UK in the mid-90s. In 1997, 2,900 people attended the first Worship Together conference in Eastbourne. The vision was always clear: not to promote one single style of worship, but to offer leaders an experience of different ways of helping people engage. This would develop into the Mission: Worship conference, held annually, which provided the perfect platform for worship leader Godfrey Birtill to lead many sessions filled with freedom, with his unique style and songs.

And there was another significant development waiting to arrive.

CCLI

This story had started back in 1983, when churches began to express their frustration at having to write to publishers for permission every time they wanted to use songs. The churches wanted to do things legally, but found it far too complicated, given that each publisher had their own rates and methods.

Geoff Shearn was in a meeting with some of the Christian publishers when the subject came up.

> That's when the idea first hit me: why don't we have a one-stop point where everybody writes in and we could issue them some sort of cover. Everybody laughed and said no way. The best that they could come up with was a somewhat begrudging agreement to say that they would all agree to standardise their charges and have the same format of form, so at least when people wrote round to different publishers there would be some level of consistency.
>
> I don't suppose anything more would have happened, except that in the spring of 1985, I was

at a Newfrontiers conference with Terry Virgo, Nigel Ring and others at Pilgrim Hall. During the break on a prayer and fasting day, Nigel saw me and said he wanted to have a chat. We went for a stroll around the grounds and he said that one of the things that was bothering them was that they were using all the songs on overheads and he wanted to know where they stood with copyright. I explained and he said 'So we're breaking the law then, aren't we?' I said yes, but that worship music was something we just had to get out and that frankly from Thankyou Music's point of view we just turned a blind eye to it, and I think most of the publishers did. I said there was a procedure for it but that it was very clunky. He said something ought to be done about that. I said it was complicated and asked him not to put pressure on the rest of the guys back at the meeting, and asked him to keep it between ourselves.

We got back to the afternoon session and the first thing that happened was that Nigel Ring got up and said he'd had a most interesting conversation over the lunch break. He asked me to stand up and explain the copyright thing. Embarrassed, I repeated what I'd said to Nigel and he said to the guys that they had all heard it and that they all wanted to do things righteously before God.

They challenged and commissioned me, as a
music publisher, to come up with a solution, and
said they would pray for me, which they did. I
felt so embarrassed, but that was it; that kind of
got the thing going and my mind jumped back to
this idea of a blanket copyright licence.

Lengthy discussions followed. Church leaders joined with
Geoff, Nigel Ring, Rob Lamont from Word Music and others.
After two or three meetings they were still no closer to fixing the
problem. The breakthrough, when it finally came, was sudden.
Geoff and Rob had a meeting with one publishing house who were
very resistant to the idea of putting copyright on worship songs,
arguing that worship should be free. The discussion seemed only
to go around in circles, but although this publishing house never
came on board, it seemed that the conversation was the catalyst
God used to finally convince Rob; a couple of days later he called
Geoff and agreed that Word would come in with Kingsway and
establish this licence.

We went live with the copyright licence in the
summer of 1985. Gerald Coates invited me up
to a private group at a weekend retreat of leaders,
where I shared about it. They asked what they
could do and I asked if they would commend it
to all their churches. It was the same with Terry
Virgo; everyone wanted to help and the licence
took off like a rocket.

They agreed that Kingsway would admin-
ister the licence, but it would be jointly owned
by Kingsway and Word. I actually had a slight
problem with that, in that as long as Kingsway
and Word jointly owned it, it would effectively
bar the other publishers, because why would
they hand their copyrights over? Although it
was successful, it was somewhat limited.

There was a need for the copyright licence to become
neutral, and in 1985, Geoff and Pat Herridge left Kingsway.
Kingsway and Word (UK) then agreed to sign the copyright
licence rights over to MGO, which was a registered charity.
Geoff changed the name of MGO to CMA (Christian Music
Association). In 1987, Howard Rachinski of the American
organisation Starpraise Ministries (who were also a church
licence organisation), visited Geoff in the UK. Geoff was then
invited to make a presentation to the US CMPA (Christian
Music Publishers Association). He succeeded in persuading
them to adopt a similar concept and encouraged them to
discuss this with Howard. Geoff and Howard subsequently
travelled around the USA visiting individual publishers. This
resulted in Starpraise Ministries changing its name to Christian
Copyright Licensing International (CCLI) and adopting the
key principles of the UK licence.

Over time, Geoff and Pat (now under the name Just Music)
provided licensing consultancy to Word (UK), Make Way Music
and Integrity's Hosanna! Music. This became more and more

difficult with the other publishers and Geoff called Howard explaining the perceptions of conflict of interests and his desperate desire to see the licence stay independent. Howard said they would do anything they could do to help, and made several visits to the UK.

Geoff went back to the British publishers to see if they would be willing to hand the licensing rights over to an independent body. Geoff explained he was willing to step down, so over a period of time that's what was agreed, and CMA handed the copyright licence over to CCLI.

The early growth was spectacular, with 9,500 churches having access to more than 200 publisher catalogues within a year of the launch. In April 1990, CCLI expanded its operation to cover churches in Canada. Today CCLI administers over 165,000 licences in Europe and 515,000 worldwide.[1]

In the history of inventions, Nigel Coltman comments, 'there are very few occasions when one person's invention remains untouched. Yet when it comes to the Church Copyright Licence, Geoff really was the one who took the concept, structured it, prepared it and presented it to the waiting world.'

Stuart Townend saw its impact. 'It's a genius thing, and thousands and thousands of writers will be eternally grateful to Geoff for the role he played in the formative years of the licence, which is a fantastic way of ensuring that writers are supported by what they have dedicated their lives to, both financially and legally. Prior to CCLI just about every church in the country was breaking the law on a regular basis and it was just a complete mess. The licence works wonderfully well.'

MISSION PRAISE

In 1984, Billy Graham led a mission to England, held in several stadiums. Graham Kendrick would lead worship at the beginning of the evening, introducing new songs such as 'You're Alive', before handing over to the worship leader from the Billy Graham team, Cliff Barrows. For these events, *Mission England Praise*, a booklet with a wide mixture of hymns and worship songs was compiled. This evolved into the *Mission Praise* songbook, which was used in a variety of church streams, especially the Church of England and the Church of Scotland. *Mission Praise* played a significant role in introducing new songs to the more conservative, traditional UK churches. The *Complete Mission Praise Anniversary Edition* was published in 2009, and included 1,250 songs.

MARANATHA

Another important opening came when Geoff and Graham Kendrick visited the Maranatha office in San Diego. Unbeknown to them it was the final day that Tommy Coombs (A&R) had to make the selection of songs for *Maranatha Praise 9*. When Graham showed up Chuck Fromm, the then President of Maranatha Music, asked if he would lead them in a short time of worship before their prayers. Geoff says,

> Graham started leading the Maranatha staff in some very simple worship songs and we spent a short time in worship. Those songs broke

something in Tommy Coombs' spirit, and he
ended up going through Graham's songs, choosing five that he wanted to incorporate in *Praise 9*.
It was only afterwards that we learned that it had
been Maranatha's policy to never use more than
two songs from any given writer.

The songs were 'Servant King', 'We Are Here to Praise You',
'Lord, Have Mercy', 'Meekness and Majesty' and 'May the
Fragrance of Jesus Fill This Place'. *Maranatha Praise* was a highly
successful series. The songs of the UK had started to leave the
islands!

Chapter 8

THE LINEAGE CONTINUES

Inspired and encouraged by the UK fathers and mothers, the younger brothers and sisters came through and flourished. This model of mentoring and training was then continued to the next generation, with each new leader releasing more responsibility to those next in line.

MAGGI DAWN

One of the leading voices at this time was Sheffield-born worship leader Maggi Dawn. Maggi played a prominent role at Spring Harvest, Worship conferences and March For Jesus events. Coming through YWAM, Maggi wrote the beautiful song 'He Was Pierced', which was recorded on the YWAM album *Tell the Nations*. Her song 'O Magnify the Lord with Me' was also recorded on Graham Kendrick's *Amazing Love* album for Hosanna! Music. Another key song from Maggi is 'I Will Wait'.

For music reviewer Sammy Horner, Maggi's music, vocals, lyrics and attention to doctrine proved that she could 'fill the shoes of any of the guys doing worship.'[1] Horner later commented, 'If worship is the lost gem of the church, Maggi Dawn continues to bring us diamonds and pearls.'[2]

Maggi had three albums released through Kingsway and has written four books. She went on to study theology and is now an associate professor of theology and literature and Dean of Marquand Chapel at Yale University.

STUART TOWNEND

In 2005, *Cross Rhythms* described Stuart Townend as 'one of the most significant writers in the whole international Christian music field'.[3] Crosswalk also commented that 'the uniqueness of Stuart's writing lies partly in its lyrical content. There is both theological and poetic expression that some say is rare in today's worship writing.'[4]

After university in the States, Stuart came back to Brighton and did a year of evangelism with Newfrontiers. Then in 1986, Dave Fellingham was recording his *In Power Resplendent* album. Stuart was invited to play keyboards and arrange the songs. This was the first worship recording that Stuart had been part of. He also sang one of the songs ('I Walk with God') on the album.

As well as becoming chief musician at Downs Bible Week with Dave Fellingham, Stuart was soon invited to play keyboards with Graham Kendrick for the Prayer for Revival events, and with Bryn Haworth at New Wine and the Vineyard conferences.

With this unique overview and involvement in different streams, Stuart was being prepared for the next role he would take up at Kingsway, of transcribing songs and editing songbooks.

Working at Kingsway gave Stuart an amazing perspective on things going on in different ministries around the world while Kingsway benefitted from having someone at the 'coal face of congregational worship' feeding back on the worship needs of the church.

Stuart's first song 'Lord, How Majestic You Are' was written in 1990, and in 1997 he recorded his first album, *Say the Word*. He has become a seasoned songsmith and wordsmith writing key songs including 'How Deep the Father's Love', and 'The Lord Is My Shepherd (Psalm 23)'. His live album *There Is a Hope* captures Stuart at his best. Stuart has led worship at Stoneleigh Bible Week, Mandate Conference and Keswick Convention. He is a popular seminar speaker, and an excellent teacher.

IAN WHITE AND LITTLE MISTY MUSIC

Between 1985 and 1992 Ian White and Little Misty Music made a most important contribution to Christian music history with the album series *Psalms Set to Music*.

Ian recorded six volumes in the Psalms series, which were expertly produced by Chris Eaton. These particularly resonated with the Scottish church, which has a heritage of the psaltry, and Ian became known as the 'Kendrick of Scotland'. He was a gifted vocalist, touring India, New Zealand, America, Australia and Singapore.

HEARTBEAT

The Psalms series was a forerunner of what was to come with the new generation, providing a more contemporary sound to the worship albums of this time. Another major contributor to the UK worship story was the band Heartbeat.

Scottish-born Ray and Nancy Goudie headed up the music department at Youth for Christ (YFC). They identified the need for a backing band to work with other YFC associated musicians like Sheila Walsh and Dave Pope. This developed into the formation of the band Heartbeat.

Heartbeat led worship on many tours and missions, and connected well with youth. They also went into schools and prisons. Heartbeat members Trish Morgan and Dave Bankhead wrote the song 'Celebrate' which was very popular at Spring Harvest. They sought to be a prophetic voice to the nation and through the project *Heal Our Nation*, made a great connection with Malcolm Du Plessis and South African record producer Joe Arthur.

Malcolm remembers:

> When we finished mixing *Friends First* I was in Cape Town and had to fly home urgently because Geoff Shearn had called and asked if I'd meet Ray Goudie who was coming to South Africa. I had a cassette copy with me and went to Durban where Ray was staying with this British couple who came to our church and were from Oxford. I walked in and said to Ray and Nancy, 'If you don't mind, I've just finished this mix and I've been on the plane, would you mind if I have a quick listen to it before we talk?' I put the cassette in and Ray Goudie went pale, because he was about to make the record *Heal*

Our Nation, but before they did it, he felt God
saying they should go to South Africa where the
next step would be revealed. The only people they
knew were Richard and Jill Lawson, so they stayed
there and Geoff Shearn had given them my name.

So when I came in and played this tape they
told me the whole story. I booked a flight and
flew with them the next day to see Joe Arthur
and then two weeks later Joe came to Eastbourne
and helped them make the record!

Heal Our Nation also introduced Southampton-born singer/
songwriter Sue Rinaldi with a quality pop voice and Su Reeves-
Bassett (who had previously sung with New Beginnings) to the
Heartbeat line-up.

Tony Cummings of *Cross Rhythms* wrote: 'Heartbeat were
spiritual pioneers pushing back the boundaries of praise music and
making Christian faith culturally relevant to a youth generation
estranged by the formality of evangelicalism.'[5] Their appearances
at Spring Harvest saw the new release of Holy Spirit praise, and in
1987 they released the single 'Tears from Heaven', which peaked
at number thirty-two in the national charts after an appearance on
the BBC's flagship programme *Top of the Pops*. The track 'The Air
I Breathe' from the following album *The Winner*, became a top ten
hit on American Christian radio.

Ray and Nancy were prophetic evangelists, and went on to
start New Generation Ministries, training up the next generation
of missionaries into the media and arts.

PHATFISH AND LOU FELLINGHAM

Dave Fellingham had had a vision for a Christian group that would be excellent musically, and be respected by Christians and non-Christians alike. Louise Hunt, who was part of TVB (The Vocal Band) at YFC and would later marry Nathan Fellingham, was invited, along with keyboard player Mike Sandeman, to become part of Purple Phatfish, in Brighton, in January 1994. For the first few years Phatfish—as they would become known—lived in Dave and Rosie Fellingham's home. In 1997 the band decided to work on some more explicitly worship-orientated songs and released their first full album, *We Know the Story*. In 1998, demos were made with producer Alan Shacklock, and Phatfish signed with US label Pamplin, and in spring 1999 *Purple through the Fishtank* was recorded with them in Nashville. Phatfish started travelling regularly to Canada, the US and Europe.

Phatfish's musical style generally consisted of a rock/pop sound utilising the keyboards and guitars and upfront vocal sound of lead singer Lou. The band always strove for musical creativity in both worship, concert and studio settings. Lyrically they sought to unpack biblical truths in an accessible way, without resorting to shallow clichés.

Reviewer Mike Rimmer wrote of the band in 2005: 'The influence of the Phatfish guys on the British worship scene should not be underestimated. Whether as songwriters or as part of the Stoneleigh worship band, they have played a major part in the last 10 years.'[6] With Nathan Fellingham as the principal worship songwriter of the band, Phatfish have contributed many worship songs to the church nationally and internationally, including 'Holy, Holy', 'There Is a Day' and 'Amazing God'. 'Holy, Holy' featured on Tim Hughes' album *When Silence Falls*.

Based at the Church of Christ the King (CCK) in Brighton, they served as the Stoneleigh band with leaders Stuart Townend and Kate Simmonds, and played a key role in all the Stoneleigh albums. They have been part of many worship conferences, leading New Songs in Nashville and Canada, as well as leading at Soul Survivor.

Lou also featured with Stuart and Kate on the Stoneleigh recordings, notably 'In Christ Alone' and 'Before the Throne'. Lou has sung on many recording sessions including the first version of 'Heart of Worship' when it was featured on the first Soul Survivor *People's Album*.

In 2006, Lou released her debut solo album *Treasure*, following up in 2008 with *Promised Land*.

On 14 and 15 March 2014 Phatfish played two farewell concerts, celebrating a significant contribution to the UK worship movement for the last twenty years.

Lou went on to record her third and fourth studio albums *Step into the Light* and *Fascinate*.

Chapter 9

SOUND OF A GENERATION

Back in the 1970s the Pioneer movement had created a culture of releasing the next generation. Most of their musicians were young. Under Gerald Coates' leadership young people were continually encouraged and given the opportunity to lead. Dave Bilbrough was nineteen years old when he led worship at the London house church movement Big Praise gatherings at the Royal Albert Hall.[1] In other movements some apostolic leaders have chosen caution, but Gerald always wanted to make room for young people whom he saw were anointed. Through this, Pioneer would increase in influence in terms of contemporary worship leaders and creativity, including Noel Richards, Cutting Edge (Delirious?), Dave Bilbrough, Sue Rinaldi and Doug Horley.

That same generous spirit had been in action in St Andrew's Chorleywood. Mike Pilavachi was in his mid-twenties when he started attending the church, and within a couple of years he was offered the role of full-time youth worker by David Pytches. Mike continued this practice:

There was one lad in the group who was thirteen, and I noticed there was something about him from the beginning. In worship, he'd be at the back worshipping his heart out. He was really passionate for the Lord, but also he looked very withdrawn in many ways.

This boy was Matt Redman, and he told me his story about some really difficult things that had happened in his life. I prayed with him, and since we both shared a passion for worship we started talking about how great it would be to go deeper in worship.

We decided that one night a week the two of us would get together in a room in the church and just worship the Lord, singing songs to Jesus for a couple of hours. I remember asking Matt what night of the week we should do and him saying, 'Well, Saturday night's the best night of the week, why don't we give God the best night?'

For a while it was bizarre. Matt wasn't that great on the guitar at that time and I certainly couldn't sing. We agreed that we wouldn't laugh at each other; we would just focus on Jesus. We would sing songs and then be still and read scriptures, pray in tongues and then pray in English. We would sing in the Spirit and sing in English—everything. After a while two or three others joined us. Looking back, I think that's

where Soul Survivor started. Before we ever had
a name, it started in that room.

As Matt and Mike were exploring the possibilities of worship,
their church leaders—David Pytches and Barry Kissell—were
wondering if there was enough demand in the UK for a conference dedicated to helping people learn about the gifts of the Holy
Spirit. In 1989, they took the plunge and hosted the first ever
New Wine conference.

Something incredible was happening with the youth in
the UK in the late 1980s. I was playing bass at the New Wine
conference at the Royal Bath and West Showground in Shepton
Mallet, as part of the worship team with Bryn Haworth.[2] One
night we went down to the youth venue, which was held in one
of the cowsheds. Mike Pilavachi was there, leading about 600
kids, and Matt Redman was leading worship. It was amazing,
God was doing so much. Each evening after our worship sessions
in the main venue I would run down to New Wine Youth to be
part of it.

For Matt Redman, attending New Wine was a transforma-
tive experience: 'I went just as a delegate first and I totally met
with God. It was a real turning point in my life. I just knew
that He was really encouraging me with a sense of His power
and I felt the strongest calling to be a worship leader. Andy Park
[from Langley Vineyard] was leading worship and he spent a few
minutes with me, and others prayed for me too.'

For Mike, the birth of New Wine was particularly exciting.
'As the youth leader of the church, when we started New Wine

I ended up doing the youth work there. Out of that I thought "Wouldn't it be great to have something like this for young people?" I went to David Pytches and said "I've got this vision to do something like New Wine, but just for young people." I thought he'd say no, but he said, "It sounds like a ridiculous idea to me, but it sounds like it might be from God so let's have a go."'

It took until 1993 for the first Soul Survivor festival to take place, and in the meantime Matt grew in confidence as he began to lead worship in the youth venue at New Wine. For Mike, those early days of Matt leading at New Wine Youth were compelling:

> It was a crazy thing because he was just a kid in the youth group. But he led and it was great. I remember just before that he'd written his first song with a guy called Paul Donnelly who was his guitar teacher at school. It was called 'There's a Sound of Singing'.
>
> At that first New Wine where he led worship, he started singing this song that I'd never heard before. It was beautiful. I looked at it and it had Matt's name on the bottom. He'd written it just a week before and it was called 'I've Got a Love Song in My Heart'. As we sang that the whole place just erupted.

The next year, in 1993, Soul Survivor started and I went to John Pac, by then Head of Kingsway, and said 'I feel there's about to be an explosion with the youth'. The Cutting Edge events—led by Martin Smith—had also just started. I suggested we start a label to facilitate that, which was different from Kingsway. I said the youth needed their own label for this time, and Kingsway allowed me to run with that. This was the beginning of Survivor Records which was set up to express the sound of a new generation.

In 1996, the first album on the Survivor label was produced. It was Paul Oakley's *Because of You*. Paul brought a bold Brit pop sound to worship and led worship at Re.vive (the youth venue at Stoneleigh) and later at Newday, the Newfrontiers youth festival. Paul also found real favour in Canada, making many trips to lead worship there, and recorded albums *Unashamed* and *Unafraid*, as well as *Kiss the River*, which was produced by renowned record maker Alan Shacklock. Terry Virgo described Paul's songs 'Because of You', 'Who Is There Like You?' and 'Jesus, Lover of My Soul' as 'magnificent', and says, 'these have gone all around the world and have been a huge blessing.' Survivor Records would go on to become more of a stable than a label. A family where young worship leaders and songwriters could develop and flourish.

In 1992 Mike Pilavachi had met Kevin Prosch, a musician and songwriter from Anaheim, California. He was pretty well known already, and everyone was singing his songs. The *Even So Come* album was a great album and he was an incredible musician. But there was something else about him; he was a prophet.

Mike felt he had a lot to teach about worship, and invited him to join with Matt Redman in leading worship at the first Soul Survivor in 1993. 'Kevin just took us places we'd never been before and Matt learned from him,' Mike says. 'Kevin affirmed and encouraged him, and then the next year the same. Gradually Matt grew in both his songwriting and worship leading skills.'

As Soul Survivor grew, other people started to notice its uniqueness. David Ruis noted that 'the amount of hunger and intrigue was great. To walk around a festival site and see the redemption of culture was a real treat. It was the broad palette of culture, not just music, and I hadn't seen anything like it at all.'

Kevin Prosch saw it too:

> Every time I went I'd always have some great talks with Matt. It was just heart to heart there. I felt there was a treasure literally in the earth. God had invested in this country. I remember seeing Matt there and telling him once 'It [the songs and the sound] will be like a shot fired around the world. The whole world will hear it—the earth will hear it.'
>
> My times there at Soul Survivor really impacted me. For the first time I felt like I had a place there—almost like a father, so to speak.

Graham Cray saw Soul Survivor up close, but also noticed the impact it was having throughout the UK.

> I personally feel that somewhere in the 80s and 90s some of it got a bit too triumphalist and a bit less vulnerable. Pete Ward has said that the emphasis was heavily on 'the Lord reigns and He has the

authority and He's coming'. I believe that with all my heart, but if you lose the power in weakness, you lose the vulnerability, the tenderness, the one another. You start writing songs in a strident style. It seems to me the newer wave that's come with Matt Redman, Martin Smith and the younger guys has got a vulnerability back in it, that just at one stage we were in danger of losing.

Soul Survivor fuelled the whole step forward for another generation. Mike has discipled and released young people with ability—obviously Matt, but also Tim Hughes and Martyn Layzell. He has released them into their gifting and worked on their character. What he's taught them is sensitivity to the Spirit. You'll still see him wandering up on stage and whispering in an ear.

The thing Mike brings is his ability to discern gifting early. The stunning thing about Soul Survivor is they spot kids with the call of God on their life and they get them to do things when they're eighteen or seventeen.

Mike spots gifting and he believes his call is to empower people and release them. What he knows about is walking with God in your weakness and being obedient to the leading of the Spirit, and he teaches them to do it within their gifting. And he knows that to mentor someone is to empower them, trust them and take the risk of letting them

try things early on. We would not be where we are
today if he hadn't done that in his youth group.

Matt didn't just benefit from Mike's mentoring. He also found
himself supported and nurtured by plenty of worship leaders a
little older than himself. As Mike recalls:

> I used to take Matt every other week around the
> M25 to Bryn and Sally Haworth's house. I would
> sit in the kitchen with Sally, drinking tea and hav-
> ing a chat. Bryn and Matt would be upstairs and
> Bryn would give Matt guitar lessons, but as he was
> doing that he was inputting into Matt all the time.
> That was incalculable. Bryn saw something, and
> he served and blessed and gladly gave of himself.
> That really spoke to me. I think what Bryn did for
> Matt has sown something in Matt; I'm not even
> sure that he recognises it. That's why he wants
> to input into other worship leaders all the time,
> because of what it did for him. They opened their
> home to us and became very dear friends. This was
> when Matt was fourteen or fifteen years old, before
> he led worship anywhere publicly.

Matt continues the story:

> When I was at university, I decided I needed
> some singing lessons. Sue Rinaldi taught me at

her house. For her to take the time out and give me that encouragement and some much needed vocal training, that was amazing.

That led on to meeting up with Noel Richards and a little group of worship leaders that he used to get together. That was great, being in an environment of people like Dave Bilbrough and Graham Kendrick. Noel was amazing to me. He spent time with me and I felt welcomed and it was just amazing to be hearing the things they were discussing and just to be part of that.

Another huge influence has been Kevin Prosch's music. I heard it on a Vineyard album and I thought it was so different to anything I'd ever heard. It seemed really prophetic and biblical and poetic. Musically it was like nothing I'd ever heard and yet it was still congregational. So that was a huge influence and we actually got close to Kevin and he ministered at some of our events. He encouraged me a whole lot and spoke into my life prophetically.

The thing is, I've had a lot of mentors—people who have taken a bit of time to give me input, and that's been the single most significant factor in knowing that I'm called to be a worship leader and going for it.

As well as meeting plenty of the more established worship leaders at Noel's forum, Matt also met two young guys from the

south coast, Martin Smith and Stu Garrard, who were just starting
to write their own songs and lead worship. They were brought
along by Andy Piercy. As Andy remembers:

> I'd known Martin through ICC when he was
> an engineer over there and I knew all the
> guys through Ishmael and the Arun Christian
> Fellowship, in Littlehampton. One time I was
> working at ICC and Martin played me a couple
> of songs he'd written and asked me to critique
> them. One was 'Thank You for Saving Me'
> and there was 'Lord, You Have My Heart' and
> 'Crucible for Silver'.
>
> Martin, keyboard player Tim Jupp and
> drummer Stew Smith told me about the meetings
> they were playing at, called Cutting Edge. They
> would worship and do Martin's songs and one or
> two others. People would give testimonies and
> someone might do a talk, and people got saved.
> It was quite new; I don't think there was anything
> else like it. It wasn't really a church service and it
> wasn't really a concert. It was a worship event that
> was evangelistic. They had great crowds coming,
> Christians and non-Christians.
>
> Martin contacted me and said they were
> thinking of making an album and would I help
> them out. They explained the money they had,
> which wasn't very much but they'd got the studio

and they had some kit and they had this limited finance so they were going to do it themselves. I said I'd love to help out because I really liked what they were doing.

My suggestion was that they forget about doing a full album and do something smaller instead, just recording the songs they really liked. We talked about it a lot and I suggested that they just did it on cassette and not CD and then sell it really cheaply.

I remember Martin's dream was that he wanted it to be a band and not Martin Smith doing this. At that time there wasn't a fixed band so we used some different musicians, but through each Cutting Edge project it progressed to being a finished band. We kept the shorter cassette format throughout, and the beauty of it was that if you do an album you do ten to twelve songs and you feel so drained at the end of it that it's very hard to get the creative flow again, perhaps for a couple of years [whereas this enabled us to record fewer songs but more frequently].

It created a real buzz and just unleashed something. I also think they learned the craft of recording really well. The first one generated some money, which we were able to put into the next one, six months later. Within a couple of years we'd produced four of these things.

They all had that feel of being underground. The idea that you just got a cassette that was really cheap and you didn't get it through a bookshop and it didn't have the standard record company name on it, meant that the kids felt that they'd discovered it and so they owned it and gave it a huge base of support.

For Martin Smith, the journey had not been just a musical one, but spiritual too:

> I was brought up in a Christian home. It was a Brethren upbringing and that connection between the head and the heart hadn't quite happened. When I moved to Eastbourne at the age of seventeen to be a trainee recording engineer at ICC I got thrown into this whole charismatic church environment.
>
> I was on a massive journey then. I wanted to discover what these people had that I hadn't. It was like this real relationship with God. I asked all the questions, and when I was nineteen I went to New Wine 1989 and I was there with my headphones on in the middle of this huge auditorium and I'd never seen anything like it. From a guy on stage very simply leading worship with an acoustic guitar, to people being prayed for and falling over.

I thought there's got to be something in this. I remember going home from that summer having been prayed for and I would say totally renewed and filled with the Holy Spirit— whatever you want to call it, I knew I'd met with God. There were no big fireworks, but I went home and spoke in tongues and the next day I wrote a song called 'Lord, You Have My Heart'. I thought 'This is the first time I've written a song like this' and 'This would sound great in the pubs'. I know it sounds amazing to say it but at that time I didn't really know the worship song scene until somebody said I should do the song at church.

Intrigued by worship, Martin decided to take a trip to California in 1991. He went to stay with a family in Anaheim, and

bumped into this long curly-haired guy who introduced himself as Kevin Prosch. He gave me this sort of knowing stare into my eyes and then two days later when I went to the church in Anaheim there he was leading worship. While I was sitting there I thought 'This is what I want to do'. Kevin was having a laugh. He was intensely spiritual, but he also was himself. He was a rock and roller and it was the first time I'd ever seen it. I thought, 'God, this is what I would love to do'. The day before I left Anaheim to fly back to England, Kevin Prosch came to me and gave me a rough mix of a new album that he'd just recorded a week before. It was going to be called *Even So Come*. He said 'Can you give this to a guy called Les Moir in England because I want him to listen to it.'[3]

Of course, I listened to it on the plane coming home and I remember crying my eyes out the whole time. I was on my way back to England and in a funny sort of way I knew I was carrying something more than a cassette to bring home. It was like God had deposited something in me and it was like a new day.

Two years later, Kevin made a trip to the UK which included leading at a prophetic music conference for Kingsway, this proved to be a significant and memorable few days. During one of the evenings of worship, Kevin stopped in the middle of the song and started prophesying over 'the young guy behind the sound desk' about his songwriting. The engineer in question was Martin Smith. Martin was soon leading worship at the Cutting Edge event in Littlehampton. It didn't take long for people to start talking about it.

> We were running Cutting Edge and we thought
> it was a high-powered youth event, doing radical
> stuff. We invited Gerald Coates and Graham
> Kendrick down to speak, and I [Martin] think at

the time a lot of people wondered why we were doing that because they were the 'old people' and we were doing a new thing. I was really adamant that we had to be in this together and that we had to honour what had gone before. I always had a sense of that with Noel, who had taken me to Spring Harvest to lead worship with him.

There was one incredibly emotional night at Cutting Edge when Graham came down and symbolically blessed me as a representative of my generation—sort of the Elijah/Elisha thing, handing the cloak on—and he gave me his jacket. Then there was me in turn blessing him and saying thank you. I remember it being an incredibly moving time. At the time I don't think people really got it, but it was something we needed to do.

Martin found himself getting to know Kevin Prosch, eventually going on tour as his sound engineer. It was yet another formative experience.

I think people need to know that there's a lot of real life going on in being fathered and if you want to get on, you've got to work hard for it and put yourself in the places where you know you've got to be. If you want to be godly you've got to hang out with godly people, and if that means driving three hours one night to get ten minutes of having a coffee with someone like that, you just do it. That's what's forming you and rubbing off on you. If it means driving two hours to London to see a gig with someone then you just do it. If it means carrying someone's bags across the world for a year, then that's all part of the process. You don't just become this songwriter or someone respected, there's a whole process.

So, yes, Kevin was a big inspiration, but looking back I was so blessed really to have so many influences. Graham Kendrick and Dave Bilbrough, Chris Bowater, Noel Richards, Neil Costello, Helmut Kaufmann, all these different influences coming my way. It was like, watch and learn and see how they do it.

Still, Kevin was special, and Martin knew it:

He was one of the first real muso worship leaders who was actually into his music. He probably wouldn't have liked the term that he was a minister, he was a rock and roller. He spent countless hours getting his guitar tones, amps, guitars, but he was inspiring and he was an artist.

That was the thing that was different. There was this fine line between him being a worship leader/prophet and him being a rock star. I think he was both. He could get up in a pub and get the whole thing going and be a rock star, or he could prophesy over twenty people in a church and totally unravel them and bring the presence of God.

That was great for me because I'd begun to live with that tension as well. I don't just want to be Graham and I don't just want to be Matt. Half of me would love to be Bono and Sting as well and I couldn't reconcile it in my own life. Can you do both? Surely one dirties up the other and this is not right?

But I knew that I had to be who I am and try and mix it all up into my life.

Martin's willingness to walk that tightrope was a benefit to others, including Matt.

Martin produced my first two albums and I found it really inspiring. You get a lot of time together in the studio, and it was partly just watching how he did things and partly when we looked at the songs together, especially my first bunch of songs—he had a lot of input there. He helped me to see how to be a bit more creative. The sound he was coming up with—there was something going on there which was pretty special. He was more like an older brother and I knew he'd tell me the truth about the songs—when he loved something and when he felt that something was not quite there.

Helmut Kaufmann, Martin's boss at ICC, was impressed by his skills.

> Martin was with us for five years and became a really good, solid engineer. He always had strong ideas and even though an engineer always does exactly what the producer wants, Martin always put his print on it. There was a sort of producer in him.
>
> There was one time when the BBC used our studio to record an extended interview with Paul McCartney as he went through the whole history of The Beatles. For Martin to get to sit in on that for three or four days [and hear Paul's story first hand] was really quite significant.

Denis Blackham mastered the first four Cutting Edge tapes. 'There was a quality to Martin's engineering, the mixes were just superb.'

Although Cutting Edge included guest musicians and singers, by Volume 4 the band line up had settled on Martin (lead vocals and guitar), Stu G (guitar), Tim Jupp (keys), Jon Thatcher (bass) and Stew Smith (drums). They didn't sign with a record company, but instead formed their own record label, Furious?. Stew was a very gifted graphic designer (then working for Anita Roddick of The Body Shop), Tim was business-minded and dealt with the bookshops. Martin recorded and worked on the records, and Stu G was playing and producing, as well as organising the tours. Jon was working on designing the website. From day one, sound engineer Paul Burton was the live engineer. Paul played a key role in the Cutting Edge sound. They were then joined by their manager, Tony Patoto, in 1997.

Martin recalls, 'It was through Cutting Edge meetings that we discovered we couldn't keep doing Kevin Prosch songs forever and realised that we had to write our own.'

The Cutting Edge events also inspired other monthly city-wide gatherings of youth including Yfriday in Newcastle, No Compromise in Chelmsford, Mannafest in Belfast and Ignite in Cardiff.

Stew Smith brought innovative design, and packaging took shape, especially in their *Live in the Can* release, their first album under the name Delirious?. A live album literally packaged in a round silver can. This caused chaos on the shelves of the Christian bookstores but started a revolution in terms of worship recording.

Louie Giglio: 'I remember where I was when I first heard Cutting Edge. While that term may often be over used, in this case it was spot on. Delirious? were the agents by which God combined a new sound (and attitude) with the new wave of worship that was emerging in the UK. Those songs sparked a torrent of creativity and still are the underlying influence of much of what we have called modern worship. Then *Live in the Can* arrived and worship was never the same.'

Wayne Drain first heard about Martin when Noel Richards brought him up in conversation.

> He said he felt like Samuel and that he'd seen
> David. He said I needed to go and see him and

the Cutting Edge thing, so my son and I went down to Littlehampton and Martin and Cutting Edge were playing by the sea.

When they started to play it was a sound that just was much bigger than a band and it shot through me. I remember telling my son that he was hearing a sound from heaven here and I said 'this sound will go around the world'. It was fresh; it was anointed and I also think it was the sound of a generation.

Chapter 10

THE 1990S—FROM STREETS TO STADIUMS

As Soul Survivor entered its second year in 1994, something new was taking place back in Toronto, Canada. People travelled to the city's Airport Vineyard Church—led by John and Carol Arnott—to experience the outpouring of the Holy Spirit known as the 'Toronto Blessing'. Thousands of Brits travelled to Toronto to experience what God was doing there, to 'catch the fire' and bring it back to Britain. This had been sparked by Ele Mumford when she came home from Toronto and shared with the leadership at Holy Trinity Brompton what God had done, and saw the same blessing being poured out.

Terry Virgo was one of those who saw the impact it was having on the nation. 'In over thirty years of Christian ministry, I had never seen anything like it. None of us had. The whole experience was totally unrehearsed and unsought. Several people were trying to stop laughing, but could not. Others tried to stand up and were similarly unsuccessful. Often, all hope of preaching was abandoned and people began to lay hands on one another to pass on the extraordinary blessing that had so sovereignly invaded these meetings. On some occasions, people had to be carried home, quite incapable of walking unaided and apparently totally drunk.'

Stoneleigh Bible Week embraced this fresh move of God, and in 1994 Dave Fellingham wrote the song 'Ruach', which went on to become the title track to the live album recorded at the event that year, reflecting what God was doing in this season, in a similar way to Paul Oakley's song at that time 'Let It Rain'.

Terry Virgo saw *Ruach* as a significant change. 'It was our first massive album. Prior to that we'd done cassettes of our worship, but they'd been kind of clunky, but this was a quality album. It also really captured the occasion. You could feel something of what was happening at the event. I think it was a superb album and it sold well all over the world.'

Stuart Townend was part of the band at the time, and was invited with them to lead worship at the Toronto Airport Vineyard.

> I look back to 1994 and I don't think I've experienced anything quite like that. Going to Toronto with the band at that time was quite amazing as well. I don't think it has had a lasting impact, but it certainly brought some of the most dynamic times of worship, when the sense of the presence of God was just astonishing. I remember leading with Dave [Fellingham] one time when John and Carol Arnott were at our church, and there was just an awesome sense of God and everybody was scared to do anything because the glory

came down. It was a time for putting down your instruments and not saying anything. We just stood there transfixed on the spot. Those were quite phenomenal times.

There was an amazing response to the *Ruach* recording. [We heard] stories of people being impacted not only during the week, but even when they heard the recording. I remember Dave Purnell [Kingsway Events Sales Manager] coming back with a story where he was working on the stand and he was playing the album and somebody fell over in the Spirit.

As Bible weeks like Stoneleigh, Soul Survivor, New Wine and Spring Harvest became bigger, a different event was being dreamed up.

In early 1994, I heard that Brazil had started to do March For Jesus. I went and was pleased to see 850,000 (according to police estimates) Christians gathered to publicly declare their faith. Whilst I was there a friend showed me a video of Brazilian Christians gathering in stadiums to worship Jesus. Something about it inspired me and when I got back to the UK I told Noel Richards about it all. He told me that God had put a similar thing on his heart, concerning Wembley Stadium.

This was not the first time I had heard about something like this. In 1991, when Graham Kendrick and I had visited Anaheim to be part of the Vineyard conference, we heard Paul Cain prophesy about stadiums being taken for worship.

Other countries were doing it too, besides Brazil. In August 1991 the Olympic Stadium in Seoul, South Korea was the venue for a three-day worship conference. It was to be the first non-sporting event ever held in the stadium, and Dave Fellingham was there.

> The grassed area was filled with dancers, reminiscent of the kind of displays which open such events as the Olympic Games. The orchestra, choir and worship leading were of the highest standard. I stood on the platform and gazed out at 80,000 people. I was so moved and excited. I could never have dreamed that one day my songs would go around the world; that God would use me to stir the hearts of his people to worship.[1]

Graham Kendrick had felt then that stadiums were going to become significant in the story of worship.

> Just because you see something coming, intuitively or prophetically or whatever, you can't always assume that you're the one who is going to do it. I was looking beyond March For Jesus and thinking 'Where does this go from here?' We kept hearing of leaders coming together who'd never worked together before and when the march was over they were saying 'What shall we do together next?' So my feeling was that this could lead to some large-scale events. I knew enough to know

that when you've got fifty leaders organising an event things can get difficult. So we tried something which involved a choir that everyone could be part of and a script which was almost like a liturgy for gathering the church and committing it to fulfil its function, 'Crown Him—The Musical'. We had one or two events in 1992 at Hereford Football Stadium, but it wasn't taken up in the way I had hoped it would.

In the Psalms we read about praising God in the great congregation, and we started to see that happening more and more in the UK. 1994 saw March For Jesus in Hyde Park, with 70,000 in attendance, part of the March For Jesus day which took place worldwide. Noel Richards, Sue Rinaldi and Dave Bilbrough led worship in Hyde Park and Graham Kendrick phoned in from Samoa, where he was leading the march there. The following year David Yonggi Cho, pastor of one of the largest churches in Seoul, Korea spoke at a gathering at Wembley Arena, next door to the famous stadium, with Noel Richards and Noel Robinson leading the worship. The event was sold out, with 11,000 people there.

It was Noel who received the clearest vision for taking worship to the stadiums. Interviewed for *Worship Together* magazine, Noel explained: 'I saw Queen live at Wembley on the television back in '86. There were 78,000 people with their hands in the air singing "We are the champions of the world", and the vanity of it all really struck me. There was so much energy in it, and yet really it meant

nothing, because it wasn't true. There's only one Champion of the
World, and that's Jesus. That's where the idea of a stadium praise
concert was birthed.'[2]

Gerald Coates was one of the first people he told:

> I used to say to him, 'Noel we are very big fish
> in very small pools. We mustn't have an inflated
> sense of our own importance or influence—we're
> not Billy Graham and George Beverly Shea.'
> Unless you're Cliff Richard and you fill Wembley
> for a different reason, as a singer in mainstream
> culture, the only person to fill Wembley was Billy
> Graham, so who on earth did we think we were?
>
> This went on for some years, with Noel
> talking about it and me thinking he was com-
> pletely off his head. One day I was sitting
> watching television with a friend from America
> and the phone rang and it was Noel saying he was
> coming round. I wondered if I'd invited him and
> forgotten, or whether we were off to a meeting; it
> all seemed a bit odd.
>
> Noel let himself in and pointed to the TV,
> saying, 'It's that, it's that!' before bursting into
> tears. My friend was saucer-eyed wondering what
> was going on. It was *Songs of Praise* in a stadium.
> That's when I realised that it wasn't some vain
> imagination of the singer singing at Wembley,
> but that this was a God-given burden.

Gerald and Noel began talking to anyone and everyone they could about the event, which was to become 'Champion of the World' and held in June 1997. Kingsway got excited and did what they could to get others involved. Engineer, producer and guitarist Neil Costello was involved in the live performances up and down the country in the build up to the event. 'I really tapped in to where Noel was coming from, more so than I did in the studio—when you go out and see people worshipping it's the music you can relate to.'

Noel had been on his own musical journey, starting with the 1993 *Thunder in the Skies* album track 'Nothing Shall Separate', which served as a signpost song for stadium anthems. After that came *Warrior*, adopting a rockier feel than his previous albums. It was all part of the vision to see the kind of music used in the recording being used at large events, particularly the stadium setting.

Neil Costello engineered and co-produced *Warrior*. 'We always wanted to try something different, so we decided to record in a big barn in the countryside. That was a significant album and it led the way for the big Wembley event.'

Noel and Gerald took Wembley Arena in 1996, which acted as a step towards booking the stadium the following year. The team found out later that Paul Cain would be able to attend the Champion of the World stadium event. I could see his prophetic word from 1991 come about, but when the day came around in 1997, things didn't look like they were going to go at all well.

In the weeks and months either side of the Wembley Stadium event, Gerald Coates had been hosting prayer meetings in Marsham Street, Westminster. 'About 7,000 people got right with

God over that period of time. The night before Wembley we were in Marsham Street and the Monday after Wembley we were in Marsham Street.' The stadium event had been soaked in prayer.

As the day approached the weather deteriorated dramatically. At one point Gerald Coates wondered whether the event would even be able to go ahead. 'It had rained all over the country for days and the great fear was that once you turned the power on the whole jolly thing was going to blow up. We were even talking about acoustic sets and some people that had come not playing.' We mobilised the intercessors to pray around the stadium, and it was decided to go ahead if possible, but with contingency plans in place. The day came and the crowds began to arrive—45,000 people, who had all driven through the rain. But when they got to Wembley it stopped and the event was able to proceed as planned.

Guitarist Neil Costello was struck by the noise of the worshippers in the stadium. 'I just remember one moment where we were singing "We Wanna See Jesus Lifted High". We had to stop playing because the people were singing so loudly and worshipping that it just took over us. We backed off and they just sang for about ten minutes. That was amazing and even now people remember it so clearly. I think we should be doing a bit more of it.'

Also part of the line-up were The Wades, Sue Rinaldi, Matt Redman, Noel Richards, Wayne Drain, Chris Falson, Delirious? and Graham Kendrick. For Martin Smith, it was significant in a particularly special way. 'It was the biggest stage Delirious? had ever played, and we were thinking "What do you do here?" Things were coming together at that point and we'd been playing a long time. We'd released "Deeper" as a single [earlier in the year], and it had gone in at number twenty in the charts. It was a bit of a buzz and it was just a huge highlight, being out there in front of 45,000 people, and hearing them sing your songs and enjoying every minute of it.'

Noel had asked Wayne Drain to join him. 'I was very honoured that Noel invited me to be with him. He's one of those guys who has the least problem with ego that I've ever met. He loves to perform; he's got the confidence to perform, but it's never about ego or pride with him. He's one of those guys who is focused on what he's doing, loves his friends and wants to do things with them. He probably doesn't realise the dozens of guys that he's given an opportunity to that they wouldn't have got otherwise, to get their songs out and to let their ministry take a higher profile.'

Peter Lyne was also there. 'Noel Richards, Gerald Coates and their team did a masterful job of pulling together a magnificent blend of musical styles, dance, prayer and testimony, during a six-hour non-stop presentation, and the sound was faultless. As one predominant Christian leader commented, it was the intensity of this new generation worshipping that was so irresistible. Such initiatives are evidence of the power of an apostolic team that successfully blends the creative and ministry gifts. They are a prophetic sign for the future direction of the church as we head into the new millennium.'

Noel had been gathering key national worship leaders bi-monthly for around three years; eating, worshipping, learning, and sharing together. The group and close community served as a catalyst for Champion of the World. At the end of the event, all the worship leaders took to the stage to worship together, singing Graham Kendrick's anthem 'Shine, Jesus, Shine'.

Record producer John Hartley remembers: 'I was there with four guys from EMICMG—Bill Hearn, Peter York, Steve Rice and Lynn Nichols. They had flown in from America and had come to sign Delirious?, which they did. But something even bigger happened as they walked in and saw almost 50,000 people worshipping God. They hadn't seen anything like it since the Jesus Movement. "America needs this," they said.'

Champion of the World was the door opener.

Neil Costello knew it too. 'I feel that something broke in the heavenlies on that day. I think the consequences of that day have rippled through the whole country and right over to America, with a new sound that definitely started up.'

One of the things that really captured the day was the video of the event directed by Stephen Bennett, who had even arranged for a helicopter to go over Wembley. He had really caught the vision for the event, and had also been key in encouraging Noel to write the event anthem 'Champion of the World'. Stephen and worship leader Chris Falson worked together in the worship team at Christian City Church in Sydney. On their wall, they had a poster of Wembley Stadium, so it was fulfilment of a dream for them to both play a significant part in the event.

After its release, the video went around the world, and inspired other stadium events to happen. Tony Patoto, manager of Delirious?, remembers 'After the success of the "Deeper" single, the video for "Sanctify" filmed at Champion of the World literally had people crying that it could happen in their own town. The diary started to fill and demands of travelling to far-away places and the partnerships of distribution and [support of our albums] went crazy.'

As always seems to happen with God, the baton gets passed from generation to generation. Just one year after Wembley resounded to the sound of worship, John Mays, then label manager for Star Song Music, played a young preacher, Louie Giglio, a video of the event. 'When I saw the Champion video,' Louie recalls, 'I knew the desires that were stirring [in me] for Passion gatherings were part of a bigger stream of global awakening. Coupled with a gathering in Seoul, these moving images helped clarify our calling and birth vision for what we have experienced through the Passion movement'.

Chapter 11

ALL AROUND THE WORLD

Even before the millennium approached, the pace of change within the world of worship had quickened. These were fertile times, and even the wildest ideas prospered as God's favour rested upon them.

In 1985 an American magazine called *New Wine* ran an article about the power of praise and worship. Mike Coleman was the president of the magazine. The response was so positive that they ran three more articles on the subject. Eventually someone wondered whether readers would be interested in hearing a tape of the actual worship.

And so began the Hosanna! Music tapes, with the team of Mike Coleman, creative director Gerritt Gustafson, marketing manager Ed Lindquist, and producer Tom Brooks.

Thirty years on and over 100 tapes later, they're still going. Will it end soon? Not according to Don Moen. 'People told us when we were on our twentieth tape that praise and worship has been "done", but look at what's happening—it's only the beginning. We distribute in about 155 nations. From the beginning that's where we've invested our time, even when it wasn't profitable. It's taken many years of sowing and working, but God has started to do something awesome. It's a real honour to be involved in something that's global.'

The Hosanna! Music tapes quickly grew into Integrity Music, and Don saw things get busy. 'There were some years where we got so busy creating products and running the company that we almost missed what God was doing around the world.' Yet they stayed true to their calling to reflect the global nature of worship.

> Our first Hillsong recording was a real turning point. Our input was minimal, and we only sent an engineer over there for the recording. It was all their production. A couple of days before the recording, I received a call from Australia and found out that the originally-scheduled worship leader (Geoff Bullock) was unable to do the recording. I was asked if I thought it would be OK if Darlene Zschech was the worship leader. I did, 'Sure, she'll do great!' Wow! It's amazing to see what God does when we put things in His control and trust Him.

Brian Houston, pastor of Hillsong Church, had a heart for worship:

> I had decided long before we ever planted a church that I wanted to build a community of worshippers that influenced other churches. I love music, but even as the profile of Hillsong Music began to grow, I always understood that

it was only because of the favour of God that, through our music, we were able to draw people into the church, and then cause them to look beyond the music to the message of the gospel.

In the early '90s, Hillsong Music had already gained credibility across the nation of Australia, and as churches sang our songs, a number of influential people in the American music industry began to take notice. People began to meet with us, and every executive I sat across from had a clear picture in their mind of what they believed would and would not work in North America. The general feeling was that in a day when Christian artists were gaining fame, the worship music of a church 'just wouldn't sell', that our style would appeal only to young people, and that we should consider adapting to a more mainstream Christian market. [...] Then in 1995, Integrity Music, based out of Mobile, Alabama, offered to distribute our music.[1]

That first album took as its title track 'Shout to the Lord', a song which Darlene said took just twenty minutes to write. 'It came out of brokenness. It was like my faith was strong but my circumstances were hard, so it came out of that.'

Though it seems strange now, to have a woman leading the live album recording was a potentially controversial decision. Yet both Hillsong and Integrity had the same passion: to simply

remain faithful to what God called them to do: worship Him
with their whole hearts, even as they confronted new challenges
along the way.

While Integrity and the Hosanna! tapes were making connections in Australia, they were also weaving their way into British
churches. Having set up both the Christian Music Association
as an independent charity and Make Way Music for Graham
Kendrick, Geoff Shearn was asked to look after the fledgling UK
office of Hosanna! Music.

Geoff remembers:

> Once I became more involved in helping intro-
> duce Hosanna! to the UK, I felt it would be good
> to introduce UK worship leaders on the series.
> We hit on the idea of taking the worship leader
> off and replacing their lead vocals with British
> worship leaders who were significant in the UK,
> including Dave Bilbrough, Dave Fellingham,
> Noel Richards and Graham Kendrick.
>
> That was the initial approach and it was a
> halfway house because the songs had already been
> pre-determined and it was very much a studio
> overdub album, not a live experience.
>
> Graham Kendrick's live recording 'Amazing
> Love' in Glasgow was the first time Integrity
> brought the whole works over, and we did the
> recording which was a genuine live recording
> with Graham leading, and with the songs having

been chosen from Graham's perspective. This was really the first full breakthrough.

Integrity Music recordings also encouraged greater integration between white and black majority churches, thanks largely to the fact that Integrity and Hosanna! had both worked with Ron Kenoly, whose album *Lift Him Up* became a classic, featuring 'Ancient of Days' and 'Mourning into Dancing'. Noel Robinson recalls:

> I came into contact with Ron Kenoly, Don Moen and Integrity Music in the early 90s and was deeply inspired and moved by this new sound of worship that suddenly appeared in the UK Christian music spectrum.
>
> These songs and choruses with their advanced musicality brought inspiration and a newness to our local church life. Years later I would find myself being the music director for Ron Kenoly as he toured the UK and Europe. It was profound that this music that was so multicultural began to shape spiritually and dynamically my generation, who were standing in the generational gap looking for the new move and expression of the Holy Spirit in our time.
>
> Ron's albums *Lift Him Up* and *Sing Out* redefined what was permissible in worship music at that time; it could never be disputed because it had the hallmark of heaven's DNA all over it. I

was deeply touched and impacted as a young black worship leader who for the first time saw a black man lead thousands of people from across the globe into deep worship that crossed cultural and ethnic barriers. This was the start of my dreams.

Another landmark recording for Integrity was *Revival in Belfast* with Robin Mark. This included the significant song 'Days of Elijah'. Then ICC label manger Adrian Thompson recounts:

> The first time I heard 'Days of Elijah' I was in my office at ICC Studios. Stephen Doherty, who at the time ran a Christian music store in Coleraine, Northern Ireland and promoted Christian events in Ireland had asked to see me.
>
> He played me some of Robin's songs including 'Days of Elijah'. Apart from the immediate affinity to Robin because of his Northern Ireland base and my knowledge of the church, CFC, where he was worship leader, something immediately struck me when I heard it. In the days when Delirious? and Matt Redman were the 'sound of the worship generation', it wasn't Robin's musical style which was more akin to James Taylor than Matt Redman, but it was the spirit that came from the songs. These songs were carrying substance that was deep rooted in Old Testament theology; apart from references to Psalms, this was

something that wasn't high on the subject list in worship. The revelation from the songs brought a fresh hope. As a worshipper, I felt something powerful off these songs and in particular 'Days of Elijah'. I can clearly remember in the days following doing a late night drive home via the M25 and being caught up in worshiping along to 'Days of Elijah'. There was an anointing on that song in particular. Something that resonated with the church. I believed this was a song I wanted to help spread to the global church.

I had no idea the significance that song would have, from being sung at the 9/11 memorial service in New York in the days following that terrible tragedy, to [being sung by] hundreds of US servicemen based in the Middle East.

It was also the song that introduced us to an alliance with Integrity Music in the USA, which opened more doors for 'Days of Elijah' to be a key song in the development of *Revival in Belfast*, a landmark album in the global worship community.

Steve Merkel who was the A&R Manager for Integrity Music observed:

As I have travelled extensively in Ireland and England, I am always grateful that there is a passion for doctrine and 'songs that matter'. As a writer myself I work hard to bring in a sense of theology and doctrine in my songs.

I think the folks in the UK have it right, in that they often don't settle for the 'flavour of the day', so it seems that songs of significance have a longer life span, much like a good hymn.

I also think that the people love to sing. I am grateful for folks who pay attention to lyrical content and the underlying theology of the songs.

Northern Ireland was also home to Focusfest, an established women's conference where the popular and inspirational Geraldine Latty would lead worship. Geraldine, gifted in leading larger gatherings, led regularly at Spring Harvest, Grapevine (now called The One Event) and Mission: Worship. She also recorded five studio albums with Kingsway Music, as well as several live projects with Focusfest.

A significant figure at this time, well recognised by her distinctive voice and role as a media communicator, was Sue Rinaldi.

Sue's life's direction had changed when her secondary school was visited by a British YFC team including Graham Kendrick and Clive Calver. Sue recalls 'They came into my school in Southampton and started to talk about God in a very different way to the way I had viewed Him then.'

Eventually she joined the YFC band Heartbeat. Sue flourished in the Pioneer movement and led worship at many conferences and festivals, including Champion of the World at Wembley Stadium.

Her albums on Survivor Records were pitched courageously at Clubland—taking worship to a new generation. A key song was 'Holy River' from the *Promise Land* album, which was produced by Caroline Bonnett.

Another distinct and diverse voice was that of the Psalm Drummers, whose self-titled album release was groundbreaking. This dazzling percussion collective took worship music into a whole new vista of creativity, a long, long way from the usual guitar driven pop rock template. The drumming visionary behind the Psalm Drummers is one of Britain's top percussionists Terl Bryant, who felt called by God to gather the drummers. Terl recalls: 'I started gathering a handful of drummers in London in 1995 and was soon hosting a regular meeting. We explored prayer and worship through drums and were really encouraged to see God touching those who came. The first four years of this seemingly "new thing" travelled fast and before I knew it there were meetings using the same name all over the UK and even some in Europe and the USA. We started a database and had over 1,500 people on it.'

Terl believes that God is restoring the drum to the church and is calling drummers, both individually and corporately to drum out a new beat, a beat that carries out the heart and inspiration of the Holy Spirit. The purpose is to declare His presence. 'I have seen drumming to be a powerful voice for prayer and praise. It can unify the divided, encourage the disheartened and stir up much-needed courage within the church in our times. Psalm Drummers is a vision where drummers drum out the beat of God's heart. It was amazing to see this tribe become a movement.'

Terl was encouraged when he visited the Drummers for Jesus gathering in Texas in 2004, where 2,000 drummers gathered for the weekend. Psalm Drummer album tracks included 'Drums of Hope', 'Rhythms of Fire' and 'Dreambeat'.

The Bible tells us that 'Where the Spirit of the Lord is there is freedom' (2 Cor. 3:17); dance has always played an important part in expressing freedom in worship.

In Romford, Christine Noble was a real pioneer in seeing dance used in worship. Dance was also a main feature at St Michael Le Belfrey. Dance team Springs were often part of the worship at Spring Harvest, and Rhian Day and Linda Lyne encouraged dance in the Scripture in Song tours and worship conferences. The early Cutting Edge events also always had dancers, led by Anna Smith.

In this area Andy Au emerged as a national leader with his unique and dramatic expression, and founded Movement in Dance (later to become Movement in Worship). Peter Lyne writes, 'When Andy dances he has an exceptional ability to interpret song and Scripture with the movement of his body, and to skilfully use banners, flags and sticks to endorse his message.'

Movement in Worship run a variety of seminars and workshops as well as a nine-month discipleship training programme. They also assign dancers to major conferences and events. Andy has overseen the dancing at many large events including Champion of the World, Wembley Stadium National Days of Prayer, Calling All Nations at Berlin Olympic Stadium, Spring Harvest and, more recently, David's Tent. Andy's unique and dramatic expressions inspire worship with his movement.

The late 90s brought an exciting wave of radical worship bands, including Yfriday and Onehundredhours.

Yfriday grew out of the Yfriday event held monthly at Newcastle City Hall and had a gritty British rock sound led by singer and guitarist Ken Riley. Their sound and songs developed well with each album, and Ken would go on to write the worship classic 'Everlasting God' with Brenton Brown. Their key song from debut album *Rainmaker* was 'Holy, Holy, Holy'.

They would record five albums, including *Revolution*, which was full of rock anthems fitting well into the British mainstay rock fraternity. Yfriday would go on to tour with Noel Richards, lead at the Grand Harvest Stadium event in Singapore, The Stand at the NEC and Calling All Nations in Berlin.

Onehundredhours were formed at The Factory in the YWAM base in Harpenden, taking their name from the Wyn Fountain book *The Hundred Hours*. With leadership from Tre and Tori Sheppard, joined by drummer Paul Baker and bass player Jono, later followed by Mark Sampson, they played and sang passionately about justice, leading at Soul Survivor, as well as in student union bars. Their song 'At the Foot of the Cross' became widely used in worship.

The attitude of worship was inherent in the Onehundredhours recordings, which included four projects. Tre claimed that 'We are a rock "n" roll band, but our heart is to worship God'. Onehundredhours had the dream to 'live with the passion that we sing'. The passion that drove them was to see worship become a lifestyle and not just a moment in a service or a fleeting feeling of intimacy. The band travelled extensively with the ministry, playing in the UK, Hungary, Norway, Finland, Holland, South Africa, Australia and the US, calling young people to a deeper level in their walk with God. In 2007 they toured the UK with mainstream artist Daniel Beddingfield.

The impact of the Champion of the World event at Wembley was noticeable, especially for Delirious?. Martin Smith recalls conversations with Sparrow Records.

> They were talking to us at that time about signing us for America, and I think they just loved the whole day and wanted to take what was happening back to America. We did a licence deal with them and we started going to America and playing at a lot of these festivals. It was another huge learning curve of how to take what God was doing in England to a crowd of 20,000 people in a field, all of them mainly being into contemporary Christian music.
>
> The first years were tough actually, trying to translate what we did into that situation. But now you see that God's done an amazing thing in the young people in America and now that's ironically what they want; they want bands to come out and lead worship. It's been amazing really. Steadily, year by year, God has done something there, and it wasn't just through Delirious? but a lot of other artists, songs and movements.

The flow of personnel back and forth across the Atlantic began to increase. Fred Heumann left the USA and moved to the UK to work for Youth for Christ, to look after the group TVB. He moved back to Nashville in 1993 and took British worship songs with him and introduced them to the New Song Church in Nashville. It was then a hugely influential church, with members including Stormie and Michael Omartian. Four years later, when Sonicflood released their self-titled first album, co-producer Dwayne Larring said 'Our track selection was taken from Fred Heumann's Sunday morning song list at New Song Church!' This album became one of the most influential modern worship albums of the time.

Speaking of the new songs coming through from the UK in the 1990s, Fred observed that

> Initially people would say it sounded awfully foreign because they weren't the chords they expected. Nashville is a city of musicians, way over-trained, way over-sensitive to melodic and harmonic differences, but the passion of the songs is what really hit. I had a sense of what God was doing with these songs, and I felt it had to come to America.
>
> We would Americanise them a bit in terms of arrangements; guys would change chords here and there. What we discovered was that the writers and people who were part of our worship team started writing like those songs. They were inspired

by them and it challenged their paradigm and the
box they were living in. That cross-pollination
produced some wonderful songs.

It's like anything else, when two oceans
collide there's some waves and turbulence, but
eventually it becomes its own entity and pro-
duces something out of that. I think we started
to see that. We were blessed to be in a church
where at one point there were 150 published
writers. That's because you're in Nashville and
that's what people do.

So in the fall of 1997 we brought over the
first Worship Together conference to Nashville.
We had Dave Fellingham, Stuart Townend and
the Stoneleigh band and some American teachers as well.

Many, like Fred, found that the worship music coming out
of the UK was a great antidote to the cynicism that can build up
when music—and worship—becomes a profession. 'Not that
it was perfect music, but it was excellent. Not that people were
without blemish, but because they were abandoned, the music
had contact. That was something we hadn't seen. Even those who
would not be as expressive in their worship as some, the more
traditional non-expressive, they could look at the content and say
"that's biblical".'

Alex McDougall was working as VP of Special Projects for
EMI, these included concept records, compilations, and marketing

worship projects. Due to a mail forwarding error, one day he received *Worship Together 4* from Kingsway, and decided to have a listen:

> When I listened to side two, I heard and sensed something that I had never experienced before. I was overwhelmed by that audio experience, and remember breaking down in tears in my office. The album included several songs by Ian White (including 'Pre-Revival Days' and 'You Are Merciful to Me'), and an ending song by Matt Redman ('There Is a Louder Shout to Come'). I listened to that little tape every day on the way to work and on the way home for weeks. I eventually made a copy of it for Steve Rice, who headed up music publishing for EMICMG. During this period, I met Fred Heumann at church, who gave me copies of the Stoneleigh band releases. I then made copies of all of the songs for our then pastor who invited Stuart Townend, Dave Fellingham and company to visit us. That was the beginning of a modern worship move in the city of Nashville.
>
> Steve Rice became a fan as well, and jointly we put together the product and marketing for the initial *Worship Together* releases by EMICMG such as *We Want to See Jesus Lifted High* which announced on the album sleeve 'Great Britain—a

land once known for its reserved religious expression has now given birth to songs and worship
leaders who are setting the standard worldwide
for powerful, progressive and prophetic songs
of praise and worship. A new British invasion is
underway: but this time it's being propelled by
God's desire to visit His people and proclaim His
glory throughout the earth.'

Craig Dunnagan former VP, Worship Resources and Marketing
at EMICMG remembers:

It was 1997 and I was sitting in my office at EMI
Christian Music Group in Nashville. At the time,
I was doing all I could to resource the songs in
our publishing catalogue and find ways to introduce them to the church. We certainly had songs
that the church could use; songs that were inspirational. However, me and a few others prayed
together on a regular basis that we would be able
to steward songs that were transformational. We
had experienced the power of God in corporate
worship and we wanted to find songs that had
the ability to carry the truth and spirit of God in
new ways.

Sparrow Records [a division of EMICMG]
had just signed the band Delirious? and now my
boss had given me some music that he had received

from Kingsway Music in the UK. The first time I put in a Matt Redman CD to listen I knew our prayers had been answered. Sitting in my office, I shut my door and began to cry as I heard songs like 'There Is a Louder Shout to Come', 'Once Again' and 'Better Is One Day'. I think I listened to 'There Is a Louder Shout to Come' three or four times in a row. I sensed that there really was a 'louder shout to come'. A new generation would raise their voice with music that they could embrace and words that could change them.

These songs weren't just sentimental. They were powerful. They were not just poetic. They were prophetic. I knew I wanted to do everything I could to help introduce the passion and truth in these songs to the church in North America. Looking back and realising the significance of those moments and the months that followed, I'm extremely grateful to have been a part of something that transformed worship as we know it. The songs from the UK sparked something that is burning until this very day across the United States and around the world.

Another North American who spent time in the UK was Brian Doerksen, whose song 'Come, Now Is the Time to Worship' was described by David Pytches as recapturing 'the spirit of the original Vineyard songs'.

We had been living in London for a few months
and one morning as I typically did I went out
for a prayer walk. Usually the focus of my prayer
was that God would call the nation of England to
worship, and raise up the people who are called to
sound the call to worship. As I was walking and
praying about this, it was like this invitation was
out there with the phrase 'Come, now is the time
to worship'. This phrase just kept on going and I
realised that all creation is sounding this call, but
God is calling us uniquely as His people to sound
the call. God was giving me the opportunity to
write a call to worship song.

I thought 'There's lots of call to worship songs,
do I really need to write one?' Then I started thinking about the things I really believe that the call of
worship is all about. Like coming just as we are. All
of that stuff. Worship is reality and one day reality
will be forced on everybody, but the most important thing is that we get the chance to choose to
worship. These things were floating around.

Under the commissioning of Ele and John Mumford, Brian did
a remarkable job of gathering key worship leaders, songwriters and
musicians from the Vineyard UK movement, and helping to refine
and shape their songs. In 1998, *Come, Now Is the Time* was released,
which acted as an introduction to worship leader and songwriter
Brenton Brown. It included some excellent songs including 'Lord,

Reign in Me' and 'All Who Are Thirsty'. This was followed up with *Hungry* in 1999, which introduced Kathryn Scott. To this day, *Hungry* stands as a turning point for modern worship.

In this season, the worship songs of the UK were earnestly championed by EMICMG in Nashville. Bill Hearn and his team caught the vision and took the songs and recordings and made them available to America. These provided many collaborations with Peter York, Brad O'Donnell, John Mays and Dave Taylor in raising the standard of recording. Steve Rice, Craig Dunnagan, Eddie De Garmo, Rick Cua, Casey McGynty, all working on publishing, Jan Cook and Christiév Carothers on artwork, and Denise George in marketing, all played a significant part.

As the partnership with America increased so did the cross-pollination of the recordings and mixes as the albums were made for the world.

From the rawer, live sound of the UK to a less ambient, more polished sound of Nashville, more and more UK albums became produced, recorded and mixed in the States.

Malcolm Du Plessis would play a key role in the Kingsway and EMICMG relationship, being a bridge and wise advisor. Malcolm would go on to spearhead the Worship Together conferences with coordinator Sue Strydom.

Englishman John Hartley, who carried the UK worship DNA, would produce many albums including Stuart Townend's *There Is a Hope*. John would go on to become A&R Manager for a few years for Kingsway North America.

Wayne Drain's perspective on the difference between the two cultures is telling.

I think some of the things that underpinned the music in Britain have nothing to do with music. Things like relationships. I think there's a local church focus that gave a certain safety to the musicians and singers, which we don't always see in the States. Usually in the States it's more about touring and selling albums, and you have to be out so much that real involvement with the local church is virtually impossible. So these young musicians and singers get out there and they're not equipped with maturity and they don't have this safety and accountability that it takes to avoid a lot of deception and temptations out there.

What I'm hoping is that the British can come in. The British music is all over the States now and I think there's at least the beginnings of a British invasion. If they can come in and talk a significant amount about relationships, about being involved in a local church, then I think the message will be complete. The concern is that the American people will take the music and probably repackage it and sell more music than you guys ever thought about. In the process we could lose the essence of what made the music so magical in the early days.

I'm thrilled that there's some partnering. If the UK can come in with encouragement and

> talking about relationships and the local church,
> plus singing these fantastic songs, I think if they
> can see America has all sorts of gifts, in business,
> marketing, all these things, and if somehow we
> can find each other and respect and learn from
> one another, I think it would be remarkable and
> we could join together to impact the world.

Kevin Prosch prophesied to me in 1994 that 'the British invasion is going to happen again and you've got three years to prepare for it.' So I knew then that there was going to be a time when the songs left the island and blessed the nations of the world.

I was at Hillsong Sydney in 2004 when Tim started to play 'Here I Am to Worship'. All 19,000 people in the room joined in singing it and Brian Houston came over to me and said: 'Supernatural song, supernatural song!' He understood that there's nothing like a God song which goes around the world, similar to 'Shout to the Lord'—it's astounding.

Darlene Zschech comments, 'The global church is far richer for the UK worship movement, and for people like Graham Kendrick who have led the way for my generation in every facet of worship ministry, seen and unseen. I feel that the UK church has such a rich history in regards to worship, that every time I am there, I come home challenged and enriched by the ministry experience.'

Louie Giglio:

> From my vantage point, a dying church through-
> out the UK was revived by a remnant cry. When

God, moving in response to people seeking a fresh wind of His life and power, began to revive His church the heart that started to beat again began to sing new songs.

Like a new spring creates a river seeking new river beds, the worship of a stirring people sought new verse and melody. Fortunately, the new never uncoupled from the rich hymnody which is Britain's past. The result was a combination of the new rooted in the old, a double-edged sword which still empowers writers like Matt Redman and others.

The music travelled with power because it was born in a revival generation. There was no worship industry, just worshipping people. The purity that resulted launched unfettered arrows of worship that have since landed on every shore.

In an interview for *Worship Together* magazine in 1994, John Wimber perfectly summed up the state of worship in the UK:

The contemporary worship that has been produced in the last thirty years of renewal in the UK is very significant. In both the mainline and house church streams, God has raised up teachers and leaders who have emphasised the importance of praise and worship, of adoration and intimacy, and this has produced the dividend of hearts ready and receptive to the work of God in the lives of His people.

I believe the best is yet to come, not only in terms of the recovery and strengthening of the church, but in the expression of that recovery and strengthening through new songs.[2]

Chapter 12

THE 2000S—THE
NEW BEGINNING

In the UK, the 90s ended with the joyful track 'Shackles (Praise You)', recorded by American gospel songwriting duo Mary Mary, being a top five hit in the official charts. This urban gospel crossover hit with a strong praise lyric and infectious groove was very popular with the gospel, R&B and pop audiences and became a dance floor anthem.

In the States, CCM (Contemporary Christian Music) remained the major attraction, and Christian musicians, songwriters and the whole industry that surrounded them were far more influenced by mainstream stadium gigs than church worship nights. In the decade and a half that followed, all that changed, as God used a series of songs to place worship front and centre.

Tim Hughes was seventeen when he first led worship at Soul Survivor. He came from a strong heritage—his father, John Hughes, was a Bible teacher at New Wine—and Tim had grown up through the New Wine and Soul Survivor ranks. Mike Pilavachi had met Tim when he was eleven years old and already saw great potential in him.

In 1999, when he was just nineteen, Tim started to write 'Here I Am to Worship'. With its hymn-like verse, cross-centred bridge and responsive chorus, this song resonated with the church and went around the world, eventually being recorded by Darlene Zschech, Chris Tomlin, Michael W. Smith, Israel Houghton, Sonicflood, and Phillips, Craig and Dean. It was declared Inspirational Song of the Year at the thirty-fourth Dove Awards (in 2003) and was the first British song to reach number one on the CCLI USA chart, going on to become number one in the CCLI charts in Canada, Australia and New Zealand too. It was a global song, and a key anthem for a generation of worshippers, paving the way for more songs from Tim including 'Beautiful One', 'Happy Day' and 'Consuming Fire'.

Tim was one of the first contemporary songwriters to express lament in worship, with songs such as 'When the Tears Fall' and 'Whole World in His Hands', from his album *When Silence Falls*, enabling the church to engage honestly and deeply with God. *Holding Nothing Back* (2007) also proved to be a landmark album which included 'God of Justice', 'Be My Everything', and 'Clinging to the Cross', a duet with Brooke Fraser from Hillsong Australia. Tim has always been a ministry-focused worship leader, and has become one of the nation's most influential worship leaders.[1]

Matt Redman's songs also continued to connect with the church, especially through his involvement with the Passion movement in the USA. 'Better Is One Day' was chosen as the theme song for the Passion - One Day gathering in 2000, and during this event Matt sang spontaneously and powerfully over America.

Matt continued to pass on his revelation and insight by writing the book *The Unquenchable Worshipper*, which went on to have an international impact. His song 'Blessed Be Your Name' (written with his wife, Beth) was also recorded by Tree63, and reached number one on the US Christian chart. It was a heartfelt song of lament, a modern-day Psalm encouraging people to worship God in the midst of struggle.

Matt's partnership with Louie and Shelley Giglio, as well as with Survivor Records, continued to grow. Inspired by the notion that 'when we face up to the glory of God, we fall face down in worship', the collaboration resulted in the 2004 recording of *Facedown* at North Point Church in Atlanta, as well as a book and a DVD. The album and DVD soundtrack were mixed in Abbey Road Studio 3 by Coldplay mix engineer Paul Hicks. The *Facedown* album cover would later be displayed on the walls of Abbey Road, next to other classic albums mixed in these famous studios.

This was an amazingly fruitful few days. As well as the album and DVD, *Blessed Be Your Name: The Songs of Matt Redman Vol. 1* was recorded, this went on to be given a Dove Award for Praise and Worship Album of the Year in 2006.

It was a wonderful season of songs emerging from the UK, which included 'Majesty' (Delirious? 2003) and 'Everlasting God', a co-write between Vineyard worship leader Brenton Brown and Yfriday's Ken Riley. 'Everlasting God' was the first worship song ever to be given an ASCAP (American Society of Composers, Authors & Publishers) award for 'Most played song by a UK writer on US radio'. Other winners of this illustrious award that year included The Beatles, Eurythmics, and Phil Collins. It was great to see a worship song recognised in this arena, reminiscent of the days of Handel and Bach, when sacred songs were the foremost music of the time.

Meanwhile the Soul Survivor festival continued to grow, expanding from 1,700 in 1993 to 30,000 in 2014. Mike Pilavachi and Tim Hughes continued to mentor and release young worship leaders such as Martyn Layzell, Vicky Beeching, Lex Buckley, Ben Cantelon, Beth Croft, Sam Bailey and Tom Smith. Along the way, the summer festivals produced some classic albums, especially *Glimpses of Glory* in 2002 and *Love Came Down* in 2006.

Reflecting the songs on the Soul Survivor album *We Must Go*, in 2004 Soul Survivor took the event to London for SoulintheCity, bringing together the themes of worship, evangelism and justice, as young people gathered in the mornings to worship God through music before being sent out to serve local communities across the capital. It all climaxed in a great gathering in Trafalgar Square, when, in beautiful sunshine, the square was filled with thousands of young people expressing their worship to God. This followed on from the pioneering Message 2000 event in Manchester, which saw Soul Survivor partner with The Message Trust (led by Andy Hawthorne). This festival combined urban action with worship celebrations and prepared the way for SoulintheCity London.

SoulintheCity became a catalyst for the introduction of a more urban style of music into contemporary worship. Thanks to the fact that London is home to more non-white churches than white churches, Soul Survivor got a little bit of a shock—in a good way—and realised they needed to incorporate the black majority church more, particularly Noel Robinson and Mark Beswick, as well as working with hip-hop bands 29th Chapter and GreenJade.

Tim Hughes' live recording of 'Shackles', with 29th Chapter rapping the verses, is still one of the Soul Survivor highlights.

It wasn't all about urban sounds, twenty-something worship leaders and new expressions of worship, though. While Matt, Tim and Delirious? were forging ahead, the modern hymn movement was about to burst into life. The ancient Celtic hymn 'Be Thou my Vision' had seen a resurgence, and 'Before the Throne', with a new melody by Vikki Cook and a contemporary Celtic arrangement by Stuart Townend, became a standout track on the final Stoneleigh album and set a course and direction for the modern hymn.

Keith Getty and Stuart Townend ably picked up the baton. They had been introduced to each other by Kingsway Label Manager Stephen Doherty at an early Worship Together conference in Eastbourne, and in 2001 wrote the richly theological 'In Christ Alone'. It was the start of a partnership that has gone on to pen many classic modern hymns, combining Getty's talent for melody with the powerful and poetic lyrics of Stuart Townend. Now, fifteen years on, 'In Christ Alone' has been translated into thirty-four languages.

The song has many fans, including Terry Virgo. 'I think Stuart has emerged now as a remarkable hymn writer, and I'm told that D.A. Carson—one of the leading theologians of our day—read out the lyrics of "In Christ Alone" in one sermon and said it was one of the greatest hymns he's ever read.'

Brian Doerksen was also impacted, a decade earlier in 1991, when he heard Graham Kendrick leading at a Vineyard worship conference. 'I distinctly remember Graham at the conference and being connected with some of what he was doing. I think what I was connecting with was the hymn-like theology in his songs, because I was raised in the church and had a real passion for theological truth in worship songs. While the intimate worship movement that was starting to happen was great, I wanted a little bit more meat, a little bit more solid theology, and I sensed that right away in Graham's music, and of course have sensed it subsequently in others from England.'

From Graham to Matt, Stuart to Tim and beyond, these writers were committed to sustaining the heritage of hymns in the UK. They wanted to offer songs of substance that were deeply infused with biblical content. Darlene Zschech remembers: 'When I started to explore worship and dig for understanding, I was amazed at the hymn-like songs that flowed from the UK, using a language that really spoke to me, *and* helped develop my theology.'

Writing with Paul Cain in the book *The Word and the Spirit*, R.T. Kendall observed that 'The greatest hymnody this century has seen has emerged from the charismatic movement.'[2]

WORSHIP AND JUSTICE

But there was one key biblical element that was often missing from our songs: justice.

It was Graham Cray who helped expose the error. Reading *The Call to Conversion* by Jim Wallis, he was impacted by the chapter that made clear the links between worship and justice. He talked with Graham Kendrick, who went on to write about the topic in one of his books. As member of the leadership team of Greenbelt festival, and Chairman of Soul Survivor, Graham Cray had plenty of potential to make a difference and he set about trying to re-establish the importance of social justice within the Christian lifestyle, worldview and Christian thinking.

Worship leader David Ruis picked up this baton, writing in his book *The Justice God Is Seeking*, 'As one who has a calling to serve the church at large by making a way for her to express worship, I cannot be faithful to my destiny in worship without wrestling continually with the place of justice in my life as a worshipper and in the life of the community in which I worship.'[3]

David pointed to the more than 2,000 Bible verses that focus on God's heart for the poor and oppressed, and reminded readers of the power behind the words Amos delivered:

> I hate, I reject your festivals
> I will not stomach your assemblies
> Even though you offer me burnt offerings
> And your grain offerings,
> I won't accept them;
> And the peace offerings of your prize beasts
> I won't approve.
> Spare me the roar of your songs;
> I won't listen to the music of your guitars.
> (Amos 5:21–23, *Postmodern Bible*)

> There is something God is looking for beyond the activity of worship, beyond the expression alone.... Worship given that does not come from a community that cares for the poor, rejects injustice and embraces generosity turns

something meant to be sweet into something very sour....

There is no true worship without community. There is no true community without embracing the poor and creating a safe space for the abused, marginalised and oppressed to find sanctuary and Kingdom justice.

The worshipping community cannot—and *must not*—divorce itself from identifying with the poor. The broken and marginalised have a central place in the identity of the church. They must not be just some distant program to which we donate money.

Expressing our faith to the society around us without the poor and oppressed at the core of that expression is to present something skewed and twisted. Just as there is no sweet fragrance for God to enjoy without justice, the Christianity we model to the world has no sweetness and our representation of the Kingdom falls short if we fail to remember the poor.[4]

John Pac also found himself inspired to discover more about the links between worship and justice, thanks to a visit to a school in a remote Amazon village with interpreter and jungle guide Gloria Santos. In her book *Wherever the River Runs*, Kelly Minter describes the moment that was to change the course of the rest of John's life:

Chief Gabriel proudly led [John and Gloria] across the village to a run-down building, with one tiny window, where approximately seventy-five children were packed in a classroom like the subway at rush hour. John was engulfed by suffocating heat and asked Gloria how hot she thought it was in the room. 'Over one hundred degrees' she said. 'This is no school'.

As Gloria made that announcement, [a prophetic word Wayne Drain had shared with John nearly a year before] appeared before his eyes like ticker tape: *It's time to release worship to the poor!* Suffering children in a dilapidated 'school' had quickened otherwise long-forgotten words. John finally understood that releasing worship to the poor had nothing to do with giving away CDs, nothing to do with songs or singing, at least not in this context. Rather, he sensed God clearly asking him to worship in a tangible way by caring for the children in front of him. The match had been struck. His first act of worship would be to build them a school so they could have an education in an acceptable environment. Though he didn't know how he'd do it, how he'd pay for it, or where it would all lead, a light in his heart and theology had dawned and its advent would change everything. For John, worship could no longer be separated from tangible acts of service that display God's justice and mercy. From

that time on, his life would be defined by that curi-
ous prophecy: *It's time to release worship to the poor.*[5]

Through subsequent visits and fundraising back home John
and his wife worked closely with Gloria in the ministry, called Ray
of Hope, and saw thirteen schools built, as well as a training and
health centre. Sadly, John died in 2013, leaving a huge hole in the
hearts of all who knew him. John believed in the power of song
to bring transformation. He also believed that a global publisher
should harvest and bring dignity to the songs and songwriters
of the nations, and strove to achieve that through his work at
Thankyou Music and Kingsway.

Interestingly, Word Records CEO Ian Hamilton would later
go on to head up CompassionUK—another record executive to
have become whole-heartedly involved in works of justice.

The roots of worship and justice stretch back for millennia,
but recent history also played its part in encouraging musicians
and songwriters to believe that they could have a part to play.
Writing in *A Desert Song*, Laurie Mellor stated:

> I believe that the profound implications of the
> Live Aid story for the future of rock music—and
> the Christian musicians involved in it—will only
> be seen in the years to come.
>
> Bob Geldof, the Band Aid single and latterly
> Live Aid (1985), this was a response of the heart
> not the mind and should be an incredible encour-
> agement to us as Christians, that the image of

> God in man is still very much alive and present.
> Rock music had never been such a powerful
> agent for good.[6]

Almost two decades on from the events that prompted Band Aid, the world watched in horror as one of the worst natural disasters of modern times struck. The tsunami that spread out across the Indian Ocean claimed over 250,000 lives and stirred compassion worldwide.

Co-founder of the London Community Gospel Choir and R&B crossover group Nu Colours, Lawrence Johnson was not content to remain a spectator. 'For the first time I felt challenged: what was I—and what were other Christians—going to do about it?' The answer was not slow in coming. Lawrence and I spoke on the phone and talked about the possibility of getting a few people from the gospel and Christian music scenes together to explore the idea of making a charity record. An hour after that first phone call I'd booked Abbey Road Studios and the ball was well and truly rolling.

That day in Abbey Road turned out to be even more significant than any could have guessed. There was one moment when all 150 artists were in the same room and we realised that we had touched something. There was a sense of these two tribes really coming together. Lawrence and I were looking at each other and we knew that we needed to carry it on.

Jointly written by Mark Beswick and Tim Hughes, the single we recorded that day, 'One Voice, One Heart', featured a great representation of British black and white singing talent. It generated

£30,000 which helped rebuild the fishing village of Thantri, south India, working closely with the charity Jubilee Action.

Inspired by his own experiences witnessing Christian work among slum dwellers in Mumbai, Martin Smith launched a bold project in 2008: CompassionArt.

Though the concept was innovative, it was also simple. Martin gathered a studio's worth of internationally recognised songwriters to join him on a retreat to write songs and sign the royalties over to charity. They all said yes: Paul Baloche, Steven Curtis Chapman, Stu Garrard (Delirious?), Israel Houghton, Tim Hughes, Graham Kendrick, Andy Park, Matt Redman, Michael W. Smith and Darlene Zschech. Chris Tomlin was ill so couldn't make the retreat, but joined in the writing and recording at a later date. The fact that all these international songwriters would gather in Scotland was a sign of the strength and standing that Martin Smith carries. The writers spent the five-day retreat at Cantle eating, walking, hanging out with each other, and documenting and recording their ideas. Joyce Meyer dropped by, and spoke with her trademark sense of humour and refreshing candour. Graham Cray led communion, and the songs flowed. Many of the songwriters had previously only written on their own. CompassionArt set a new model and formed a safe place for cross-cultural collaborations. Worship leaders from around the world became friends. People fell in love with working and writing together.

Tim Hughes remembers: 'It was amazing to sit in a room with people like Graham Kendrick, Michael W. Smith and the others and see how they approach songwriting, and learn from that. I want to give more of my time to doing this and I want to learn from others. There's the sense of making a stand for those who have nothing, just really affirming God's heart for the poor, the broken, and that actually as a church we have to play a part in that.'

A couple of months later, the team reassembled at Abbey Road Studios to record the album. Guest vocalists included Amy Grant, Leeland Mooring, Kirk Franklin, Toby Mac, CeCe Winans and Joel Houston. The Watoto Children's Choir also featured on the album, having been recorded by Martin Smith in Kampala, Uganda.

CompassionArt placed worship and justice at its core and smashed the single songwriter model. This template has now been used around the world, where songwriters gather together and collaborate on songs coming from creative communities.

NEW INITIATIVES

Ken Costa, Chair of Alpha International was intrigued that many worship leaders were heading out to Hereford to complete their albums. The engineer they were going to work with was New Zealander Sam Gibson, who had found a wife as well as a home at Chapel Lane Studios, and soon became the go-to guy in terms of mixes for the modern worship sound.

Sam's first key album mix was Delirious?'s *World Service* (including the song 'Majesty'), in 2003. This was followed by albums by Hillsong, Tim Hughes, Soul Survivor, Rend Collective, Bethel, Kari Jobe, and Jesus Culture. Sam has made an important contribution to the sound of worship albums.

The year 2008 saw the merging together of ICC and Spring Harvest, two organisations that had been working together for nearly thirty years on a number of initiatives, including Spring Harvest music products. Alan Johnson, Chief Executive of Spring Harvest, said 'This merger gives Spring Harvest and ICC Media Group a great opportunity to combine their creativity and to develop further the range of exciting resources they have been producing in recent years for the church both here in the UK and around the world.'[7]

Peter Martin, Chief Executive Director of ICC said 'For many years the close working relationship between Spring Harvest and ICC Media Group has been truly unique and probably one of the strongest in the Christian world. Our vision is to create an organisation that will better equip the church with resources to help it maintain its cutting edge in a rapidly changing society. We can achieve this more effectively operating together rather than separately.'[8]

Meanwhile, things were changing at Kingsway. The successful book and curriculum company David C Cook based in Colorado, USA, had owned fifty-one per cent of Kingsway for some years. Finally, in 2010, it acquired 100 per cent of Kingsway as well as Fierce! Distribution (whose artists included Cathy Burton, Verra Cruz, Switchfoot, Graham Kendrick and Bluetree), originally set up by Delirious?. This meant that the Fierce! Managing Director, Jonathan Brown, and staff members made the move to be part of Kingsway, and signaled a period of expansion for the company as it moved into North America. Within a year, David C Cook also acquired Integrity Music, changing its global music brand name to Integrity Music and appointing Ryan Dunham as president of the new expansive and progressive company.

ENCOUNTERED, EQUIPPED AND EMPOWERED

In 2006 Tim Hughes and his wife Rachel had moved to HTB. Tim joined worship leader Al Gordon, and in 2008 they founded Worship Central together, to help resource local church worship teams to 'Encounter God, equip the worshipper and empower the local church'. They worked under the umbrella of Alpha International, the evangelistic course that has been completed by over twenty-seven million people worldwide. Tim and Al were soon joined by Soul Survivor worship leader Ben Cantelon, and the team grew to include Luke and Anna Hellebronth, Nikki Fletcher, Nick Herbert, Daniela Hogger, Tom Read and Tom Smith. To date, Worship Central have recorded three classic albums; *Spirit Break Out*, *Let It Be Known* and *Set Apart*—each one containing songs whose impact went far beyond Britain, especially the song 'Spirit Break Out' which was championed by Kim Walker-Smith of Jesus Culture, and recorded by William McDowell. 'The Way' was also featured on the Passion album *Even So Come*. The song 'Set Apart' also inspired over 100 gatherings of worship teams during January 2015 from London to Mumbai, Vancouver to York, meeting anywhere from living rooms to cafés to churches. It was a significant way to begin the new year, coming together to 'set apart' an evening to worship God, have fellowship, prayer and prophetic ministry, consecrate themselves and commit to seeing the worship of Jesus Christ made central in society again.

Taking inspiration from Alpha, Tim and Al established the Worship Central course. Free to download, it has currently been translated into twelve languages and run in over 110 countries more than 5,000 times, reaching 62,000 worshippers. Tim Hughes explains, 'The vision I have with Worship Central is to see every church with an incredible worship leader who is anointed, gifted and humble.'[9] Elsewhere he says, 'Worship Central seeks to empower the local church and we want to see thousands of worship leaders raised up to lead. It's about sharing an idea and a group of values and dreams to see Jesus glorified and the church alive in worship'.[10]

While Tim was building a team in London, Matt Redman was also building something new: a songwriting partnership with Jonas Myrin from Hillsong. 'You Alone Can Rescue' (2008) was Matt's first co-write with Jonas. In the years that have followed it has proven to be an incredible writing combination. It has enhanced Matt's ability to write poetic lyrics that are filled with just the right imagery, and this song in particular showed that Matt felt free to write in a more hymn-like way than before.

It has been quite remarkable that Matt has been able to sustain this level of songwriting for so long. Some songwriters hit a golden patch, which lasts a few years, but Matt is still going strong. Twenty years after 'I Will Offer Up My Life', he and Jonas wrote '10,000 Reasons'.

Even though '10,000 Reasons' came quickly, in a way it had been brewing for a while. I remember visiting Matt's house and seeing a bookcase of old hymn books. I knew that he was studying hard, trying to understand the heritage of hymns and working out how to join that to the knowledge of what God had called him to do.

I don't think that there's another song this decade that has resonated with the global church like this one. From funerals to prison executions,[11] '10,000 Reasons' has helped to draw out praise in the midst of some of the most painful and fearful situations imaginable.

While Matt continued to hone his songwriting craft, the world of worship took some new twists and turns, one of which was the end of Delirious?'s time together as a band. This climaxed in their farewell concert in 2009 at Hammersmith Apollo, after playing in over fifty countries, with global album sales of 2.5 million units, and distribution in ninety-six nations around the world. Although the evening was marked with mixed emotions, it celebrated God's faithfulness and the journey from Cutting Edge to *Kingdom of Comfort*. It was an unforgettable evening.

Northern Irish band Rend Collective took on the baton from Delirious? with a fresh, organic sound bursting with creativity and energy. They went on to find favour in America, touring with Chris Tomlin and eventually moving to live there, while still remaining a well-loved part of the Soul Survivor family.

Martin Smith went in a different direction after the end of Delirious?. He started to record his own projects collaborating in the international worship community, and wrote new songs with Chris Tomlin and Nick Herbert, including 'God's Great Dance Floor', and 'Waiting Here for You'. In 2011, Martin and Tim Hughes worked on Tim's studio album *Love Shine Through*, featuring the song 'At Your Name' (co-written with Phil Wickham). He also went on to record the classic *Live in New York* album with Jesus Culture, released in 2012. 2009 also saw Matt Redman receive the

ASCAP award in Nashville for Christian Songwriter of the Year. As Matt and Martin Smith wrote in their song 'All Over the World':

All over the world Your song will resound
All over the world Your praises ring out
We're living to see Your name and renown
All over the world.

EPILOGUE
What is the Future of Worship?

2015 saw the recording of Matt Redman's *Unbroken Praise* album in the world-famous Abbey Road Studio 1. Filling the most famous studio in the world with worshippers and worship teams from around the UK—and inviting Louie Giglio to bring a message into this temple of sound—offered a perfect picture of how far the world of worship has come over recent decades.

Fifty-five years have passed since A.W. Tozer made his observation about the missing jewel. As I write these words at the start of the summer of 2016, it's worth noting that from May to August, around 225,000 Christians will gather at British conferences and festivals, united by worship.

The BigChurchDayOut (brainchild of ex-Delirious? keyboard player Tim Jupp) has become big news, with over 30,000 attending in 2016 and plans to go to two sites in 2017.

Would Tozer be happy? I'm sure he would. Would he say that the jewel has finally been found, that worship is no longer missing from the church? Take a look around you and I think that the best is yet to come.

Local churches, cells, congregations and celebrations are becoming ever more dynamic, and I believe that we're witnessing the restoration of the Great Assembly. I think this will lead to more stadium events—like Calling All Nations in Berlin Olympic Stadium where Noel Richards gathered worship leaders from many nations to serve Europe. The Call Worldwide and Global Days of Prayer are also gathering the church together to worship and intercede for their nations.

The complexion of the UK church is changing. The African church is now the fastest growing church stream in Britain, and with its growth come new sounds and rhythms as worship becomes more multicultural. The Redeemed Church of God (RCOG) was founded in Nigeria in 1952, and is now in 180 nations with 700 parishes in the UK. African worship leader Muyiwa Olarewaju has become the most prominent worship leader in the UK African church alongside Ghanaian Sonnie Badu. The RCOG take over the Excel Centre in London twice a year for the Festival of Life, an all-night gathering of worship and prayer attended by 40,000 people.

UK church leader Pastor Agu Irukwu of Jesus House was named Britain's most influential black person in 2011, and he has been part of major London gatherings with Nicky Gumbel (HTB) and Gary Clark (Hillsong London). Ruach, led by Bishop John Francis, bought Kilburn Gaumont, the largest cinema in Europe, and are now seeing it filled with worshippers each Sunday. These are exciting times in the Church of England, too, and under the leadership of Archbishop Justin Welby, the Anglican church is advancing.

Look back to Acts 2 and you'll see that Pentecost painted a picture of a future where people from different cultures are attracted by hearing their own heart language and are drawn in to worshipping God as a result. I believe we will hear the sound of every tribe, tongue and nation worshipping together on earth as in heaven and that the multicoloured church will display the manifold wisdom of God. Kensington Temple in Notting Hill, London, provides a prophetic picture as every Sunday people from over 145 nations gather to worship God together.

As the jewel has become a light to the nations, it's been wonderful to see what God is currently doing in Europe. The ICF church planting movement, which started in Switzerland, is spreading rapidly, and writing songs that will be sung across the continent. The This is the Day event in Budapest is seeing over thirty nations gather in the László Papp Sports Arena. Holland and Germany are also seeing great congregations come together to worship God. I believe Europe's destiny is even greater than her history.

New Christian TV and radio stations continue to spring up across the UK and it is now normal for millions to see and hear passionate, powerful worship on the BBC's *Songs of Praise*. The *Dance Again* testimony and song, from Life Church, Bradford has also had ten million views on Godtube.

The landscape is also changing as the influences upon worship shift from the south of England up to the midlands and the north of the country. As I write, the Worship Central team have moved from London to Birmingham, not far from where the UK leaders for the Vineyard Church are based, in Nottingham, or from one of the most influential Newfrontiers churches in

Bedford. A little further north and Life Church, Bradford stands as a city on a hill, while the courage and bravery of the Manchester church leaders is becoming contagious as it connects more to the UK church. Kingsgate Community Church has sprung up in Peterborough and Causeway Vineyard is thriving in Coleraine, Northern Ireland, seeing a wonderful move of God. Ffald y Brenin in South Wales has become a place of blessing, while City Church in Aberdeen, Scotland is growing so fast it currently fills nine separate venues.

As more churches around the country are being planted by mission-minded teams, the training up of worship leaders has become vital. As a result, more and more worship academies are springing up.

There is greater collaboration and mixing of the streams as songwriters make new connections at city-wide worship gatherings. Kingdom Come is proving to be a nation-changing event, providing evenings of worship and intercession, prophetic flow with passionate prayers for revival. The recently established David's Tent event is seeing thousands gather to spend three days in God's presence as worship and prayers continue non-stop, fulfilling the mandate of seeing the restoration of the tabernacle of David.

Bethel, Jesus Culture, Hillsong and Gateway have also provided role models and been an inspiration in terms of releasing women worship leaders. This has fuelled the UK female worship leaders as they move confidently into their calling. One day, soon I hope, they really will break through the stained-glass ceiling.

The lineage of Levites will continue with a new generation breaking through and bringing new energy; young lions, wild and pure hearted, untamed from conforming to respectable church behaviour. The current ceiling is their floor. New songs will be written from fresh revelation about subjects yet to be explored.

In Psalm 40:3 we read:

> He put a new song in my mouth,
>   a hymn of praise to our God.
> Many will see and fear the LORD
>   and put their trust in him.

I believe that we will see more music missionaries travelling out to the nations, as well as an increase of others coming to the UK. There will be more and more worship highways built; not out of cement and steel, but out of worship songs that travel around the world. We'll see more and more indigenous worship songs translated into English, revealing to us the breadth and power of God's worshipping church.

I also believe that modern hymns will continue to resonate with people, meeting their desire for more substance in songs. Worship leaders will be like storehouse owners; learning to bring out treasures old and new (Matt. 13:52) as they find a balance between content and engagement.

Instrumentation will continue to become more diverse with more instrumental music as musicians are released to play. When that happens, healing often follows.

Speaking a few years ago at a Worship Central conference at Westminster Central Hall, Nicky Gumbel spoke out prophetically:

'The next move of God in evangelism will be led by the musicians. In front of the army will be the singers and musicians. Songs will change the nation. Songs will call prodigals back home into the church. Let's impact the mainstream music scene and society.'

In October 2014 Cindy Jacobs also prophesied:

> The Lord said to me today, 'Psalm 133, United Kingdom, red, yellow, brown, black and white, dancing upon injustice, releasing the Glory of God to the streets'. God has brought the Nigerians and the people from the West Indies. Some people say the complexion of the nation has changed, but the Lord says 'I have caused it to be the colour I have always wanted it to be in my people coming together as one, for love has no colour.' The Lord says 'Do not fear that you will lose who you are, for I am going to loose the Spirit of evangelism, I am going to begin to move upon those, and I am going to win them to me, I am going to woo them. Those who you have most feared I am bringing for the greatest harvest this nation has ever seen.'
>
> A sound is going to be released that is going to be greater than anything that has ever come out of this nation before. God says, 'I am going to raise it up, I am going to raise up a new generation with a new sound that is going to pierce the heavens and release this anointing to her destiny.'

Perhaps one of the clearest pictures came in the form of a song by Delirious?, 'Did You Feel the Mountains Tremble?'

And we can see that God You're moving
A mighty river through the nations
And young and old will turn to Jesus
Fling wide you heavenly gates
Prepare the way of the risen Lord

Open up the doors and let the music play
Let the streets resound with singing
Songs that bring Your hope
Songs that bring Your joy
Dancers that dance upon injustice

I see this as a prophetic statement of the future of the jewel of worship. I believe that there will be more worship on the radio, more worship flowing into film soundtracks and a glorious renaissance as the walls between sacred and secular are broken down.

Brian Houston, speaking to a journalist for an Australian newspaper, was asked about the Hillsong Live church album being at number one in the mainstream chart. He said that 'it was great to see that worship of Jesus was the most popular music in Australia today.' This is an inspiration for all of us concerned about worship. I believe this will happen in nations around the world.

I believe that community has always been a core value for us as musicians, and I believe that it will continue to be at the heart of the UK worship scene. In my mind, community is the only way that we can ensure we find a healthy balance between the tension and opportunities of becoming an industry. Community leads to collaborations; collaboration leads to innovation. Darlene Zschech comments, 'Oh how I love the worship community in the UK. It feels like family. Fathers and sons, mothers and daughters … shared wisdom and rich heritage.'

Mike Pilavachi believes that the thing that is unique to the UK is unity and favouring one another, and lack of competition, as well as commitment to being part of local church:

> That's a big thing. It's not that it doesn't happen anywhere else and that it happens completely here, but it seems to happen more here. Also because the worship has been rooted in the local church, whether it's the Anglican church, Pioneer church, Vineyard church, or Newfrontiers church, there's freshness and an anointing on it. The worry I have is that we turn worship into an industry and it becomes this parallel universe to the local church. That's why I've loved it that we have had a partnership with Kingsway because it's been a partnership where the Christian record label has been working with the leadership of the local church to serve the local church. That's what we've got to fight to keep and to guard. If we end up with just a bunch of itinerant so-called musical worship leaders that are not rooted in the local church, we'll have lost the plot completely.

But above all, there is one simple reason why the last few decades have been so fertile for worship in the UK, as Brian Doerksen makes clear:

> I think one of the reasons that British worship has such favour is because in embracing the new modern worship, they have not turned from their ancient roots. There's a sense of clarity in the message and what the lyrics are about. A lot of the Brits seem to have this anointing to write about the cross and these amazing theological truths and yet they package them in this fresh, youthful, not overly produced or glossy way.
>
> God is still honouring the promises He made to Britain in the last several hundred years: the calling that Britain has to bless the nations of the earth, the calling that Britain has in a sense as an originator—the language of English that is the media pathway through radio and television. It's almost like you've been given a trust and then God has put in a seed of worship and now it's blossoming and it's bearing fruit and the nations are eating of that fruit and being satisfied by it. I think it's inevitable—God is fulfilling the promises He made.

LIST OF INTERVIEWS

This book is the culmination of many interviews conducted by the author with the following key contributors to the story of the UK worship movement. The interviews were variously conducted in person, over the phone and via email and have in some places been edited for flow. I am very grateful for the time each of these gave me for this project.

Mark Beswick	Jean Darnall
Mike Bickle	Brian Doerksen
Dave Bilbrough	Wayne Drain
Chris Bowater	Malcolm Du Plessis
Terl Bryant	Craig Dunnagan
Clive Calver	Dave Fellingham
Gerald Coates	Peter Fenwick
Nigel Coltman	Louie Giglio
Barney Coombs	Jeanne Harper
Neil Costello	John Hartley
Graham Cray	Jack Hayford

Chris Head   Andy Piercy
Fred Heumann   Mike Pilavachi
Sammy Horner   Kevin Prosch
Tim Hughes   Beth Redman
Ishmael   Matt Redman
Lawrence Johnson   Sue Rinaldi
Helmut Kaufmann   Dave Roberts
Graham Kendrick   Noel Robinson
Phil Lawson-Johnson   David Ruis
Pete Meadows   Geoff Shearn
Steve Merkel   Martin Smith
Don Moen   Maurice Smith
John Noble   Stuart Townend
John Paculabo   Terry Virgo
John Pantry   Darlene Zchesch
Tony Patoto

TRIBUTE TO JOHN PAC

January 2013 saw the sad loss of John Paculabo (John Pac).

Since joining Kingsway in 1988 John had worked hard to establish Kingsway's worship song copyrights. Under John's stewardship, Thankyou Music became a global song publisher, realising his dream to 'see the worship songs of the UK leave the island'.

John encouraged the worship community to champion songs of substance, 'songs that when heard carry a biblical curriculum wrapped up in three minutes'. He truly believed Thankyou Music was stewarding the songs that would be sung for centuries to come.

Here are some tributes from good friends of John:

EDDIE DE GARMO (PRESIDENT OF EMICMG PUBLISHING 2002–2014)

John Pac was a dear friend in every way a friend can be. He was my teacher, my mentor, and a true visionary. Even more than those lofty things, he was my buddy. We loved to hang out together, talking about anything and everything. We discussed our children, our wives, and our businesses. The conversation always came back around to building God's kingdom, because that was what was ultimately dearest to John.

MATT REDMAN

John Pac had a brilliant mix of business brain and kingdom heart. He worked hard to build up a music company that would reach far and wide across the nations, and God established the works of his hands. It's hard to estimate just how many lives and churches have been impacted by these endeavours. In later years John was entrusted with another ministry—Ray of Hope—a work of kindness among the people of the Amazon. In effect, Ray of Hope has been the sweet-sounding harmony that accompanies the melodies being made at Kingsway. It is worship and justice flowing hand in hand—such a powerful and profound combination. Through Kingsway, Ray of Hope and of course through his inspiring family, John Pac has left an amazing legacy.

MIKE PILAVACHI

John was unique. He was a pioneer, a visionary and an entrepreneur. He saw the future before the rest of us and brought that future into the present. As CEO of Kingsway he brought together a team who impacted the worship of the church around the world. He believed in young worship leaders like Matt Redman and Tim Hughes and put the resources of Kingsway behind them. We can forget now just what vision that took. In all his roles, he was always willing to innovate and always ready to change direction when he saw the need.

As Paul told the Corinthians 'You have ten thousand teachers, you do not have many fathers'. John was one of those fathers whose faith, vision and encouragement influenced not only our own lives but many around the world.

CRIS DOORNBOS (CEO OF DAVID C COOK)

Thank you, John, for inspiring the works of writers whose songs have touched untold millions of believers worldwide. We celebrate your invaluable contribution to these songs that will continue to serve as foundational hymns of the church, sending a message of a saviour resounding through centuries and countless generations as yet unborn.

NOTES

CHAPTER 1

1. A.W. Tozer, *Worship: The Missing Jewel in the Evangelical Church* Volume 2 (Pennsylvania: Christian Publications, 1997, Audio Book).

2. See Ephesians 3:16.

3. Stuart Townend and Les Moir, 'The Musician in Revival' an interview with John Wimber, *Worship Together* (Kingsway, 1995), 4.

4. See Bruce Welch, *Rock 'n' Roll—I Gave You the Best Years of My Life: A Life in 'The Shadows'* (London: Viking, 1989).

5. Joy Webb, *Bridge of Songs* (Norwich: Page Bros, 2000), 6.

6. Brian Houston, 'The Church I See', *Worship Leader* (November/December 2013), 50–51.

7. Terry Virgo, *No Well-Worn Paths* (Eastbourne, UK: Kingsway, 2001), 86.

8. Andrew Walker, *Restoring the Kingdom* (London: Hodder & Stoughton, 1985), 36.

9. Onyekachi Wambu (ed.), *Empire Windrush; Fifty Years of Writing about Black Britain* (Great Britain: Victor Gollancz 1998), back cover copy.

CHAPTER 2

1. Ralph Turner, *Gerald Coates Pioneer* (UK: Malcolm Down, 2015), 77.

CHAPTER 3

1. Graham Kendrick and Clive Price: *Behind the Songs* (Stowmarket: Kevin Mayhew Ltd. 2001), 33.

2. Kendrick and Price, *Behind the Songs*, 39, 49–50.

3. Kendrick and Price, *Behind the Songs*, 66.

4. Kendrick and Price, *Behind the Songs*, 8.

5. This is a saying describing being able to write a catchy song using just three chords.

6. Album review by Dave Roberts in *Christian Music Association Magazine*.

7. James Attlee, 'Dave Fellingham: Worship Music's Author, Composer, Musician and Pastor', *Cross Rhythms*, 1 July 1990, www.crossrhythms.co.uk/articles/music/Dave_Fellingham_Worship _musics_author_composer_musician_and_pastor/36279/p1/.

8. Tony Cummings, 'Bryn Haworth—More Than a Singer', *Cross Rhythms*, 1 July 1992, www.crossrhythms.co.uk/products/Bryn_Haworth/More _Than_A_Singer/5611/.

9. Laurie Mellor, *A Desert Song: Christians in Rock—A Spiritual Battlefield?* (Rustington: Slim Volumes, 1987), 61, 62.

CHAPTER 4

1. Quoted in Laurie Mellor, *A Desert Song: Christians in Rock—A Spiritual Battlefield?* (Rustington: Slim Volumes, 1987), 46.

2. Paul Northup: *Thirty* (UK: Greenbelt Festivals, 2004).

3. Teddy Saunders and Hugh Sansom, *David Watson: A Biography* (London: Hodder & Stoughton, 1992), 163–64.

4. Bazil Meade and Jan Greenough, *A Boy, A Journey, A Dream: The Story of Bazil Meade and the London Community Gospel Choir* (Oxford: Monarch, 2011), Recommendations.

5. Philip Mohabir, *Building Bridges* (London: Hodder & Stoughton, 1988), 126–27.

CHAPTER 5

1. Dave Roberts, 'Calling All Nations', *Worship Together* 27 (May–June 1999), 17.

2. Andrew Walker, *Restoring the Kingdom* (London: Hodder & Stoughton, 1985), 308.

3. Walker, *Restoring the Kingdom*, 309.

4. Graham Kendrick, Gerald Coates, Roger Forster and Lynn Green, *March for Jesus* (Eastbourne, UK: Kingsway, 1992), 126–28.

5. 'March for Jesus', *Wikipedia*, https://en.wikipedia.org/wiki/March_for_Jesus.

6. Walker, *Restoring the Kingdom*, 362–63.

CHAPTER 6

1. This was an anecdote John recounted in many talks over the years.

2. Terry Virgo speech at John Wimber's memorial service, Westminster Central Hall, Spring 1998.

3. David Pytches, ed. *John Wimber: His Influence and Legacy* (Guildford: Eagle, 1998), 63.

4. Quoted in Pytches, *Wimber*, 69.

5. Andrew Walker, *Restoring the Kingdom* (London: Hodder & Stoughton, 1985), 311.

CHAPTER 7

1. See CCLI website: http://uk.ccli.com/about/.

CHAPTER 8

1. Sammy Horner, 'Maggi Dawn—Follow', *Cross Rhythms*, 1 October 1993, www.crossrhythms.co.uk/products/Maggi_Dawn/Follow/6462/.

2. Sammy Horner, 'Maggi Dawn—Elements', *Cross Rhythms*, 1 February 1997, www.crossrhythms.co.uk/products/Maggi_Dawn/Elements/6461/.

3. Tony Cummings, 'Stuart Townend: The Worship Leader and Hymn Writer', *Cross Rhythms*, 28 March 2005, www.crossrhythms.co.uk/articles/music /Stuart_Townend_The_worship_leader_and_hymn_writer/14571/p1/.

4. Debra Atkins, 'Song Story: "In Christ Alone"' Crosswalk.com, 22 July 2004, www.crosswalk.com/church/worship/song-story-in-christ-alone -1275127.html.

5. Tony Cummings, 'Heartbeat: Charting the History of Britain's Pop-Evangelists-cum-Praise-Band', *Cross Rhythms*, 1 August 1991, www.crossrhythms.co.uk/articles/music/Heartbeat_Charting_the _history_of_Britains_popevangelistscumpraiseband/36498/p1/.

6. Mike Rimmer, 'Phatfish—Faithful: The Worship Songs', *Cross Rhythms*, 1 March 2005, www.crossrhythms.co.uk/products/Phatfish/Faithful _The_Worship_Songs/12300/.

CHAPTER 9

1. Church leader Maurice Smith has been credited as commenting that they only took the Royal Albert Hall because his front room wasn't big enough!

2. Until this point, my knowledge of the story has been mainly through books, interviews and conversations, but now I began to be part of it as a musician, an engineer and later an A&R manager.

3. Kevin and I had already met in Anaheim a few years previously when I was musical director for Graham Kendrick at a Vineyard worship conference.

CHAPTER 10

1. Dave Fellingham, *To the Praise of His Glory* (Eastbourne, UK: Kingsway, 1995), 15.

2. Dave Roberts, 'Calling All Nations', *Worship Together* 27 (May–June 1999), 17.

CHAPTER 11

1. Brian Houston, *Live, Love, Lead: Your Best Is Yet to Come* (UK: Hodder & Stoughton 2015), 38–39.

2. John Wimber, 'The Musician in Revival', interview conducted by Stuart Townend, *Worship Together* (September 1994).

CHAPTER 12

1. Recognising the place and role Tim would play in this country, Martin Smith gave him the title 'Mr England'.

2. Paul Cain and R.T. Kendall, *The Word and the Spirit* (Eastbourne, UK: Kingsway, 1996), 79.

3. David Ruis, *The Justice God Is Seeking* (California: Regal, 2006), 21.

4. Ruis, *Justice*, 44, 45

5. Kelly Minter, *Wherever the River Runs* (Colorado: David C Cook, 2014), 56–57.

6. Laurie Mellor, *A Desert Song: Christians in Rock—A Spiritual Battlefield?* (Rustington: Slim Volumes, 1987), 62.

7. 'PRESS RELEASE—18 MARCH 2009: After 30 years of partnership, Spring Harvest and ICC Media Group "Join the dots"' Memralife group, www.memralifegroup.org/downloads/2009-03-18_Memralife_Group.pdf.

8. Press Release, Memralife Group, 18 March 2009.

9. Tony Cummings, 'Tim Hughes: The Contemporary Worship Man Talks about "Love Shine Through"', *Cross Rhythms*, 9 March 2011, www.crossrhythms .co.uk/articles/music/Tim_Hughes_The_contemporary_worship_man _talks_about_Love_Shine_Through/43004/p1/.

10. Mike Rimmer, 'Worship Central: Tim Hughes and Al Gordon Talk about Worship Movement', *Cross Rhythms*, 5 October 2011, www.crossrhythms .co.uk/articles/music/Worship_Central_Tim_Hughes_and_Al_Gordon _talk_about_worship_movement/44595/p1/.

11. Craig Borlase, 'The Bali 9, Executed As They Sang 10,000 Reasons' We Are Worship website, 25 January 2016, www.weareworship.com/uk/blog/matt -redman-reflects-on-the-bali-9-executed-as-they-sang-10000-reasons/.